OUR HEADS ON STRAIGHT

SOBER-MINDEDNESS—A FORGOTTEN CHRISTIAN VIRTUE

MICHAEL PHILLIBER

White Blackbird
BOOKS

PRAISE FOR OUR HEADS ON STRAIGHT

"Refreshing" is the word that pops into my mind for Michael Philliber's *Our Heads on Straight*. I tire of reports and books that imply that we need to panic—the church is in another emergency. Instead, Philliber calls us to sober-mindedness—not somber-mindedness, not Down-in-the-mouthville—but to steadiness, to sanity, and all-in a Gospel-grounded, Bible-anchored way, looking to a character-changing result.

Dale Ralph Davis

Author, Former Professor of Old Testament at Reformed Theological Seminary, Retired minister

We live in the time of plague. A coronavirus has sickened and killed millions. But spiritual plagues—polarization, conspiracy theories, hatred, and violence—have taken their toll on us as well. Philliber's fine book delivers a challenge and an opportunity for the church to be sober minded in this unstable world, to stand apart from the mayhem, and to point the way to Christ.

William Price, PhD

In a world that seems "out of its mind," Dr. Philliber's book comes at the right time! In an overly anxious culture, a bit of sober-mindedness would go a long way. Dr. Philiber takes what we already know (what Scripture says) and reminds us that its power, principles and practicality can help lead the way for us to find a richer trust in our storm-calming savior, thereby finding that desperately needed sober-mindedness.

Paul G. Rebelo

Pastor, Chapel Hill UMC

We live in a world that has found a personal justification for every wrongful suspicion and an echo chamber for every conviction. In *Our Heads on Straight*, Mike traces out the Biblical roots of sober-mindedness. From there he sketches out the present consequences of a lack of sober-mindedness, but also the remedy available in Christ. We would all be better from reading this book and reflecting on our own heart in such a contentious age.

Zack Carden
Pastor, The Church of the Apostles

There are a multitude of Christian books today on how to pursue successful lives, families, and churches. Perhaps even more on how to have an impactful, meaningful walk with Christ. Many of these books are good, but they can also cause us to feel a constant strain, a constant burden to do more. With their strong exhortations and specific applications, these books can bring a restlessness that causes us to put zeal before knowledge so that we end up doing more harm than good. What if we slowed down and instead tried first to learn better how to think as Christians? What if we slowed down to try to evaluate all these endeavors in the light of Christian wisdom? What if we learned once more what it is to be sober-minded?

That is the challenge that Micheal Philliber takes up in his latest book, "Our Heads on Straight: Sober-mindedness, a Forgotten Christian Virtue." As an Air Force veteran and Presbyterian pastor with decades of experience, Philliber has the maturity and wisdom to instruct us how we might recover this forgotten wisdom so often missing from Christian discipleship. And in case we think this is some ivory-tower exercise, Philliber applies sober thinking to a wide variety of "hot-topic" issues, including sexism, racism, and our use of social media. As a model of sober-minded thinking, he begins with the problem, and then uses Scripture to instruct us on wise and sober ways we might approach such difficult issues. This is something we can all grow in, no matter how long we have walked with Christ. As the old confession of sin puts it: "Grant, O most merciful Father, that we may hereafter live a godly, righteous, and sober life, to the glory of thy holy name. Amen." Philliber's book helps us to do just that.

Christopher Hutchinson
Pastor, Grace Covenant Presbyterian Church Author, *Rediscovering Humility*

In this timely and accessible book, Michael uses both technical arguments and stories to remind us of the virtue of sober mindedness. Calls to virtue are hard, because airtight argument isn't enough—example must follow. In Michael the reader will encounter a humble and encouraging teacher who walks the walk and shares how to do the same.

Stephanie de Oliveira Chen, PhD

Through this book I learned that there is a lot more to being sober minded than meets the eye. Pastor Philliber does a fantastic job in expanding the meaning of sober mindedness and shows us how we can apply it in our lives today.

Jasmin Rodriguez
Historical European Martial Artist

CONTENTS

FOREWORD AND ACKNOWLEDGEMENTS

It was a pleasant season. Heritage Presbyterian Church in Oklahoma City sent me off to enjoy a sabbatical from the middle of September to the middle of December 2019. My wife and I enjoyed our time away. We hiked in Oregon, camped, visited the Grand Canyon, and more. During this rest, I pulled together the book that sits in your hands.

Once I completed the work, I began two tracks. I started looking for a publisher, a process that can be disheartening. I also taught this book as a class for my congregation from January until March 2020. I was encouraged by the feedback and felt confirmed in my train of thought.

But this was before COVID-19, BLM, protests, mask and anti-mask tensions, QAnon, big C conspiracy theories, hot political divisions, and the presidential election of 2020. During all of the brouhaha of that year, I continued looking for a publisher who might value the prescient value of the book. I watched, listened, and experienced much that this book addressed and was meant to amend.

I was happily encouraged by several in my congregation to get it published because they felt it was just the right book at the right time. Therefore, I was delighted when my friends at White Blackbird agreed to print this manuscript. I am grateful for the opportunity they have afforded me. I'm also deeply appreciative to Stephanie Chen, John McNeely Hudson, Christopher Hutchinson, and a host of others who read an earlier copy of this work and gave me wonderful advice.

And most especially, I say "Thanks with hugs" to my wife, who gave me the space to write this work and was my sounding board.

INTRODUCTION

Sobriety

I once ran a correctional facility in the US Air Force. Nothing big or glamorous, just a low-grade facility that housed residents for thirty days. It was their last chance in the Air Force. If they messed up after their time with me, they would be discharged. Most of my occupants had received non-judicial punishment, called an Article 15, for alcohol-related incidents. This means that I had to march them to the Social Actions detachment to be interviewed by the Drug and Alcohol counselors. After a few months of doing this, I became close to several of these counselors. Some of them had serious alcohol problems in their past but were now working on staying clean and helping others. They would often advocate that my Airmen should attend Alcoholics Anonymous (AA) weekly, and I would have to arrange for them to be escorted to meetings. It was during this time I concluded that I ought to see what AA was all about, and I'm glad I did.

While attending various AA meetings, I gained a ton of insight from "the Old-Timers," those men and women who had been sober quite a long time. For example, the old-timers wouldn't allow participants to play emotionally manipulative games. They had no problem seeing through the facades and calling people to task if they were blame-shifting or being down-right rapscallions. Further, if a man or woman had abstained from alcohol but was still trying to control or manipulate others, was ruled by their anger, or blamed someone else for all their problems, the old-timers called them "dry drunks." They enlightened me to the difference between a drunk—with all his stinking thinking—who was only abstaining from the drug-of-choice and someone who was genuinely working on his sobriety. It was this experience with "Bill's friends"[1] that began to pique my perspective that there was a distinction between those who stopped using and abusing their drug-of-choice and those who were really working on themselves, their attitudes, and their relationships. A woman might not be drinking, but she could still be acting out her abusive behavior and abrasive actions; or she could be abstaining and working on living soberly. These old-timers gave me a new category to think through: sobriety is more—much more—than being simply "dry" or abstaining from an addictive drug.

Those experiences were back in 1986–1989. After that, I moved on, finished my associate's and bachelor's degrees, and half of my seminary degree. Then I retired from the Air Force, completed seminary, and became ordained in a conservative Presbyterian denomination to serve in local churches. But I have never forgotten the categories those old-timers gave me.

During the following decades of ruminating and Bible reading, it dawned on me sacred Scripture presents something of a similar framework. I started observing that Holy Writ, specifically the Greek New Testament, used a word-family, *sophroneo*, in a smattering of locales which conveys more than the notion of being "dry." It appears to pick up what those AA old-timers meant by a life of sobriety. This word is translated in multiple ways, such as

—"temperate," "sensible," "wise," "prudent," "self-controlled," "sound minded," and so forth.

As I dug deeper, it became clear that this family of Greek words with their synonyms, and in their contexts, were important. As a result of where the *sophroneo* words come up and how they are placed, I began to realize that Paul, Peter, and the gospel-recorders—the only ones who used the words—picture the Christian life as a life of sobriety.

From an example outside of the Scripture, the biblical concept is fittingly expressed in the concluding request from the classic Anglican confession of sin: "And grant, O most merciful Father, for his sake, that we may now live a godly, righteous, and sober life, to the glory of your holy name. Amen."[2] The use of these words means more than remaining "dry" and moves further out into the ways of our thinking and acting that are wholesome and healthy—personally, relationally, and socially. And so, I decided to write this book to help reclaim the qualities of sober living.

At this point, I need to fill up some sandbags and place them along the bank to assist in holding back a potential flood of concepts. To do this, I will take a brief trip over into a select number of historical and linguistic subjects. If language and history are not your idea of fun, you can skip this next section and move on to the closing two paragraphs of the introduction.

Sandbags

To help us set up some boundaries, I will sketch out how the *sophroneo* word-family was used and understood in classic Greek, with the aid of Adriaan Rademaker and his doctoral thesis, *Sôphrosyne and the Rhetoric of Self-Restraint: Polysemy and Persuasive Use of an Ancient Greek Value Term*. Next, we will see how this word group carried over into the Septuagint, specifically in an addition to Esther, as well as Wisdom and 2 and 4 Maccabees.

Finally, we will take a quick glance at where it shows up in some early pastors and theologians of the late-first and early-second centuries. Although one could potentially bring out a few semantic changes in the use of this vocabulary as time rolled by, nevertheless the main aspects of the *sophroneo* family of words seems to hold steady.

Classical Greek

Rademaker dug deep into several major classic Greek works such as Homer, Aeschylus, and Plato, to see how *sophron, sophrosyne*, and their cognates were understood and used. This long and labor-intensive study found that the words were polysemous—they had a variety of meanings and implications. The areas of definition were slightly different based on the object's class, age, and sex. For girls and women, it normally indicated quietness and seemliness, even marital fidelity. For young men and boys, again the notion was quietness, along with order and decentness. For slaves, order and obedience. For the *polis* (city), there should be good order and sound judgment.

Finally, adult men carry the largest weight by exhibiting respect for the gods, lack of violence, not being unjust, and exhibiting quietness, moderation, measuredness, sanity, and prudence. In the end, Rademaker compiled the multifaceted definitions and inferences into a broad swath of general categories that fall under *good sense*. The good sense to avoid harming oneself or others, and the good sense to avoid indecency and disorder. In classical Greek, the *sophroneo* words carried the idea of prudence, decency, quietness, and soberness in a way that related to the control of desires.[3] How did these terms fare in later years, especially as used in the Septuagint?

Septuagint

The Septuagint (often abbreviated by the Roman numerals LXX, for seventy translators) took the Hebrew scriptures and translated them into Greek. None of the *sophroneo* words are used to translate any Hebrew vocabulary. But there were a few extra documents and segments that came straight into the LXX as Greek, often known as the deuterocanonical books or apocrypha, which do use the words. The value of looking into these texts is to see how the meaning was changing or refined within a Hellenized-Jewish context. There are only a few places where this *sophron* language surfaces.

To begin, there were Greek additions to the story of Esther. In those supplements the term is employed once. In 3:13c, it is in the description King Artaxerxes writes about Haman. There he declares that Haman is a man "who excels in soundness of judgment (*sophrosyne*) among us, and has been manifestly well inclined without wavering and with unshaken fidelity."[4] In this line, the expression continues to convey the thought of good sense and discretion.

There is also the Wisdom of Solomon, in which "Solomon" is praying for wisdom in the ninth chapter, extolling wisdom's value. Upon arriving at verse 11, we read, "For she knows and understands all things, and she shall lead me soberly (*sophronos*) in my doings, and preserve me in her power."[5] Wisdom is pictured as the guide and guard. As a guide, she leads seekers with good sense. The word is used as a positive quality that fits in with the classical Greek notions from earlier years.

Further, in 2 Maccabees, there is an account of Onias' death. Antiochus hears of it and is grieved because "of the sober (*sophrosynen*) and modest (*eutaxian*) behavior of him that was dead."[6] Sobriety and modesty, or orderliness, sit together. In 4 Maccabees chapters 1 and 2, *sophrosyne* and *sophron* begin to appear in lists of the excellent qualities of right reason and the characteristics of wisdom. For example, in 1:18, "the forms of wisdom are prudence (*phronesis*), and justice (*dikaiosyne*), and manliness (*andreia*), and temperance (*sophrosyne*)."[7] Here, the term is swimming in the same pond of traits that are lived within social contexts. It's not just a state of mind, but a way of embodying that state of mind. Finally, in chapter 4, the word is coupled with a more cognitive phrase, *sophron nous* (temperate understanding or thought).

From the uses of the terminology in the LXX, the ideas of good sense, controlling and restraining desire, prudent conduct, and orderliness from the classical period remain. Likewise, this is seen in the company that the *sophron* words keep, such as prudence, modest behavior, and others. This brings us to briefly and loosely note how these terms are classed in the earlier church after the New Testament texts were written.

Apostolic Fathers

The expression "apostolic fathers" is shorthand for Christian pastors and theologians who wrote in the immediate years after the New Testament authors faded from the scene. It's a short span of time from the end of the first to the earlier years of the second century AD. The vocabulary we are focusing on is used by both Clement of Rome and Ignatius of Antioch.

Very early in Clement's singular letter to the Corinthians, he takes note of their faith and piety: "For who has ever visited you and not approved your highly virtuous and stable faith? And not been astonished by your temperate (*sophrona*) and gentle piety in Christ?"[8] Though they are not completely synonymous, temperance and gentle piety walk along with a highly virtuous and stable faith.

Then, toward the end of the letter, Clement summarizes what he has written and places our term in the middle of a list of character traits that go hand-in-glove with other wholesome qualities. He writes:

> For we have touched on every aspect of faith, repentance, genuine love, self-restraint (*egkrateias*), moderation (*sophrosyne*), and endurance, reminding you that you must be pleasing, in a holy way, both to the all-powerful God—by acting in righteousness, truth, and patience, living in harmony, holding no grudges, living in love and peace with fervent gentleness, just as our ancestors, whom we mentioned before, were pleasing to God by being humble minded toward the Father, who is both God and Creator—and to all people.[9]

Further, Clement characterizes the couriers who carried his letter to Corinth. He describes them as "faithful and temperate (*sophronas*) men who have lived blamelessly among us from youth to old age."[10] Finally, this pastor ends with a prayerful blessing that God might:

> Grant to every soul that is called by his magnificent and holy name faith, reverential awe, peace, endurance and patience, self-restraint (*egkrateian*), purity, and moderation (*sophrosynen*), that they may be found pleasing to his name through our high priest and benefactor, Jesus Christ.[11]

In Clement of Rome, the *sophron* words continue to express the perspective of good sense and a quality of life and faith that attends it. The same can be said of the way Ignatius of Antioch employed these terms in his letter to the Ephesians and Philippians. As he writes to the Ephesians, he points out how *sophrosyne* is part of imitating Jesus Christ and resisting the devil, "… with all holiness and self-control."[12] Lastly, the bishop reminds the Philippians that widows are also to exercise "self-control" (*sophronousas*) "with respect to faith in the Lord."

From this short historical and linguistic survey of pre-New Testament sources (the classical Greek and Septuagint) as well as the post-New Testament apostolic fathers, we gain a stronger sense of how the *sophron* words were employed, and the various aspects they implied over multiple generations. Though it may be possible to tease out a few semantic changes in the use of this vocabulary through the centuries, the main aspects appear to have remained. The ideas of good sense, controlling and restraining desire, prudent conduct, moderateness, and orderliness persist. By examining the longer history of the terminology, we have a better and firmer handle on what we are looking at when we enter the New Testament. Which brings us to the shape of the present book.

Shape

My plan in this book is to show the significance of *sophroneo*, its cognates, and its main synonym (*napho*) in the New Testament. From there, I will display why this is a consequential virtue, and the various ways it is meant to express itself in our lives as followers of Jesus. Therefore, the first chapter will plant us securely in the Gospel by taking us to an important episode in the life of our Lord. By the end of the first chapter, I hope Christians will have a renewed confidence in Jesus and how he is the source of sober-mindedness.

For those readers who have never embraced Jesus as he is freely offered in the Gospel, it is my prayer that they will come to do so.

The second chapter will examine Titus 2:1–14 and make the case that sober-mindedness is an important value that all followers of Jesus should desire to grow in. Once that is accomplished, chapter three will pick up Romans 12 and move toward encouraging us to practice sober-mindedness in "normal" times and situations as a way of habituating good sense. The fourth chapter will set out how and why sober-mindedness is richly beneficial in the "abnormal" seasons and situations by hearing God speak to a prophet in Isaiah 8:11–13. These studies will be background for the last five chapters, which are intended to guide readers away from joy-destroying doom and gloom toward a stronger confidence in the storm-calming Savior.

The volume's title is significant in keeping us on track—*Our Heads on Straight: Sober-mindedness, a Forgotten Christian Virtue.* To begin, we turn to two episodes in the life of Jesus that go closely together. These have impacted my whole evaluation of *sophron* and what a life of sobriety, of being sober-minded, denotes.

---

1. Regular attenders of AA call themselves "Bill's friends," referring to the founder of AA, Bill Wilson.
2. The Anglican Church in North America, *The Book of Common Prayer 2019*.
3. Rademaker, "Sophrosyne."
4. Elpenor, "Septuagint."
5. Ibid.
6. Ibid.
7. Ibid
8. Loeb Classical Library 2003, *Apostolic Fathers 1*, 1:2.
9. Ibid., 62:2.
10. Op. Cit., 63:3.
11. 10:3.
12. 4:3.

STORMY SEA AND STORMY SOUL

THE SHAPE OF SOBER-MINDEDNESS

Lord, this I ask, O hear my plea,
Deny me not this favor:
When Satan sorely troubles me,
Then do not let me waver.
O guard me well, My fear dispel,
Fulfill Your faithful saying:
All who believe
By grace receive
An answer to their praying.

—Preussen, 1554

Two scenes in Jesus' life have arrested my perception of what it means to be sober-minded. These true, factual accounts are full of hope and good news. No matter the storms one is slammed with, Jesus' "Peace! Be still!" can liberate the fearful and fettered. I'm referring to the stormy sea and stormy soul in Mark 4:35 through 5:20. Open a copy of the Bible or an app and take a moment to read this segment before you go any further. These two scenarios go together to give listeners and readers a solid sense of storminess and fear while showing us the One who calms and conquers storms and squalls.

Stormy Sea

If you've ever experienced a storm, you can get a clear sense of what's going on here. Since I live in Oklahoma and grew up here, I have stories about being outside in gales, thunderstorms, tornados, and the like.

But at least I had solid ground under me. I can only imagine what it would be like to sail along in a large boat, and the next thing you know, the waves are crashing over the sides, the wind is whipping up a squall and screaming at you, and your vessel is pitching this way and plunging that way. Nothing is steady and nothing feels solid. That's the situation here. Mark writes, *"And a great windstorm arose, and the waves were breaking into the boat, so that the boat was already filling"* (Mark 4:37).

At this point, you must give the disciples a smidgen of credit. They brave the gale long enough to hunt down Jesus sleeping in the stern of the ship, *"And they woke him"* (4:38b).

I'm sure it was something like the plane ride I had once. I was flying to Shepherd Air Force Base in northern Texas to meet a man who wanted to be a medical professional in the Air Force. I was sent to give him a tour of his first assignment. In the seat across from me was an off-duty pilot heading out to start his workday. The small twin-propeller commuter plane took off and gained altitude.

Things were going fine until it suddenly felt like I was riding a bucking bronc! We would ascend in a jolting, rocky fashion then abruptly drop what seemed like a hundred feet. This continued for quite some time, and my stomach was up in my throat. I began to get worried that we were going to crash until I happened to glance over at the off-duty pilot calmly reading his Wall Street Journal. I immediately thought, "Well, if this pilot's not worried, neither should I be." It was small comfort, but it was comfort!

Once the disciples find our Lord and awaken him, their desperation rings out as they say to him, *"Teacher, do you not care that we are perishing"* (4:38c). It's an impossible situation, and Jesus is sleeping! What!? Yet, instead of turning on them and chewing them out, Jesus *"awoke and rebuked the wind and said to the sea, 'Peace! Be still!' And the wind ceased, and there was a great calm"* (4:39).

First, our Lord addresses the impossible situation by speaking a two-word command (in the Greek) to the chaotic creation, "Peace! Silence!" and all was still, with "a great calm." Just two simple directives and the chaotic creation rests content. The raging ruckus settles down, and sensible order is restored.

Then Jesus addresses the incredulous disciples with soul-searching questions that jump off the page and begin to speak to us: *"He said to them, 'Why are you so afraid? Have you still no faith'"* (4:40)? How often those two questions from our Lord's lips have hounded me. They're not "smack-down" questions but the kind that challenge us to examine our hearts, our orientations, our worries, and the reasons behind them. The One who can speak two words and creation hushes invites us to trust him with our destiny, our direction, and our deliverance.

Finally, the followers respond to Jesus' actions and words. Observe that this reaction comes as a result of both our Lord's command to the stormy sea and the doubt of the disciples: *"And they were filled with great fear and said to one another, 'Who then is this, that even the wind and the sea obey him'"* (4:41)? If they were afraid of the chaotic creation before, they are even more frightened by the one who simply turns the storm into calm with two words! And their question also lingers with us, demanding from us a reply: "Who is this?"

Here is where we ought to pause and take a moment to think

through our answer to that question, which I encourage you to do before you move forward.

But I must press on.

The stormy sea episode was surprising, and hopefully faith-inspiring. But now we slip on over and engage with the stormy soul.

Stormy Soul

I'm guessing that the disciples' legs were a bit rubbery after enduring the stormy sea. It must have felt nice to reach shore and stretch their legs. But they weren't there long before things got upended. We read, *"immediately there met him out of the tombs a man with an unclean spirit"* (5:2). It doesn't take much to find out what this unclean spirit was that seems to have had hold of the man (5:9). A raging regiment of demonic forces is using the man and making him a stormy soul. As we walk through the narrative, it becomes apparent that the man—physically, emotionally and psychologically—is under duress and in distress.

He comes forth from the tombs (5:2) where he lived (5:3).

This is a place that is startling. And it is hugely unnatural.

Most people in their right mind would find other places to abide, but the man dwells among the dead and decomposing. This unnatural dwelling place indicates that he was alone, separated from social connections and relationships. It is equally abnormal to dwell among the dead and decomposing and away from a living community. The Creator once stated, *"It is not good that the man should be alone; I will make him a helper fit for him"* (Gen. 2:18). Even the sacred sage observed, *"Whoever isolates himself seeks his own desire; he breaks out against all sound judgment"* (Prov. 18:1). Jesus and the disciples meet this rugged individualist, this solitary man, dwelling alone with the raging regiment, all eerily unnatural.

Further, he was unrestrainable. We read:

And no one could bind him anymore, not even with a chain, for he had often been bound with shackles and chains, but he wrenched the chains apart, and he broke the shackles in pieces. No one had the strength to subdue him. (5:3–4)

Somehow, the locals had been able to capture him on past occasions. Maybe out of fear for their own and his safety, they had sought to hold him down and bridle him. But it all proved undoable because he even broke the shackles into shards! Though the narrative may be emphasizing a strange superhuman strength, it seems better to see the accent falling on the lack of control, unable to be controlled by others coupled with his own inability to govern himself. Notice: *"...no one could bind him... wrenched the chains apart... broke the shackles.... No one had strength to subdue him"* including himself. He was unrestrainable externally and internally.

Not only did he exhibit what was unnatural and show himself to be unrestrainable, but he was also unsettled. Mark writes, *"Night and day among the tombs and on the mountains he was always crying out and cutting himself with stones"* (5:5).

There was no calm or quiet for him, because the raging regiment troubled him to the point that there was no stopping him. The physical effects would have exacerbated the situation. For example, without a regular amount of REM (rapid eye-movement) sleep, a person becomes susceptible to depression and has a hampered emotion regulation which then opens the door to various psychological disorders.[1] This man was without peace or rest, constantly on the move. He was running off into the tombs and trekking up the mountain, constantly in motion and continually on the go. And as he did this, he howled while taking up stones to harm himself. His unsettledness not only gave him over to restlessness but also worked into self-destructive deeds.

Here was a manic man doing what was unnatural. He was unrestrainable and unsettled. He was isolated from others, dwelling among the dead and decaying, always on the go, lacking self-control, unable to be constrained, and harming himself all along.

It must have been harrowing to meet this man. In many ways his existence was ruled by hysteria. He needed grounding, orderliness, and sobriety.

But there's hope coming because this stormy soul is about to experience the one who brought peace to the stormy sea.

It is interesting that this manic man, this stormy soul, ruled as he was by the raging regiment—*"when he saw Jesus from afar, he ran and fell down before him"* (5:6). Something about Jesus drew this man across the rock-strewn, tomb-riddled mountainous terrain to come and fall at Jesus' feet. He came to the One he felt was disturbing him. We read: *"And crying out with a loud voice, he said, 'What have you to do with me, Jesus, Son of the Most High God? I adjure you by God, do not torment me'"* (5:7).

This stormy soul had it all backwards The torment was coming from within himself. The One he had come to was setting him free, but he couldn't see it that way: *"For Jesus was saying to him, 'Come out of the man, you unclean spirit'"* (5:8)!

Then, after finding out the name of the forces that had this man in its grip (*"My name is Legion, for we are many"* 5:9), the raging regiment begged Jesus that they might move their battalion headquarters to a herd of swine in the area. They begged the One who could command the stormy sea with two words and reign it in. They begged, Jesus "gave them permission" (5:13), and they packed up and shipped out immediately.

There is hope here for any who are captured by their unnatural existence, those who are unrestrained and unrestrainable, those who are unsettled, even trying to destroy themselves. Jesus gave the demonic battalion permission, and they pulled up stakes and scurried off leaving the manic man behind.

This episode reminds me of when I was a hospice chaplain in another state. I would regularly visit the inpatient hospice house, going from dying patient to dying patient. One day I went to see a man who had been a successful minor league baseball player. He was only in his early forties but had been consumed by alcohol to the point he was now a few days away from death. The alcohol and resultant physical consequences (liver, brain, etc.) had affected his cognitive abilities. He could barely speak, and he was often unintelligible.

I sat with him for a few minutes, hoping that somehow my words could penetrate the fog. I mentioned how we often have demons in our lives that get hold of us and rage within us. Though I'm certain that demons exist, I was simply speaking metaphorically. But I was shocked to see him push himself up and turn to me roaring some garbled noises, looking at me with what appeared to be pleading eyes! I was truly taken aback. I immediately began pointing out how Jesus has liberated many who were dominated by other forces and had broken their power. That in his death and resurrection, we can not only find forgiveness but also real freedom.

He laid back down, I prayed with him, and left him with a biblical promise. I have no idea if he turned to the Lord for deliverance and absolution since he died two days later, but I do hope God did more with my measly words than I could possibly have crafted or conceived.

Once the swineherders ran off to the closest city and reported what they had seen and heard, the locals came rushing out *"to see what it was that had happened"* (5:14). And what they saw made them respond in fear (5:15). Just as the disciples responded to Jesus' actions with fear (4:41), so the city folk did likewise. Jesus' mercy, grace, and liberation strikes fear in the hearts of many. We sing:

> *'Twas grace that taught my heart to fear,*
> *and grace my fears relieved;*
> *how precious did that grace appear*

the hour I first believed![2]

Unfortunately, and a bit surprisingly, the city dwellers beg Jesus to leave them (5:17) because they have become disconcerted by what he was able to accomplish.

But the greater surprise is in what the urbanites observed, the very thing that discomfited them: *"they came to Jesus and saw the demon-possessed man, the one who had had the legion, sitting there, clothed and in his right mind, and they were afraid"* (5:15). Here was the manic man, the stormy soul, and he was no longer stormy. Mark shows us how completely changed the man had become by using three participles in the Greek.

First, for all of his one-time restless rambling and racing, going and blowing day and night, now he was purposefully sitting. He was seated up close to his storm-calming Savior. He was seated and at peace, no longer agitated and no longer driven to roar and howl and destroy himself. In the words of the old hymn:

> *All the way my Savior leads me;*
> *what have I to ask beside?*
> *Can I doubt his tender mercy;*
> *who through life has been my guide?*
> *Heav'nly peace, divinest comfort,*
> *here by faith in him to dwell;*
> *for I know, whate'er befall me,*
> *Jesus doeth all things well.*[3]

Not only was he sitting peacefully—he was also now clothed. His immodesty must have been the result of his ragged existence before, and it is now remediated. But even more, his self-destructive scars and bruises were covered over, clothed. The Greek word gives the impression that someone else clothed him, and he was the passive recipient of being clothed by another. Like when Adam and Eve after they had been driven from the Garden because of their rebellion. Yahweh does not leave them naked and ashamed. Nor does he allow them to head out wrapped in their wilting self-remedy. Rather, God covers their nudity and ignominy with animal skins (Gen. 3:21). So here the man has found covering for all the marks of his disgrace and degeneration. This picture is echoed in the words we sing:

> *Nothing in my hand I bring,*
> *simply to thy cross I cling;*
> *naked, come to thee for dress;*
> *helpless, look to thee for grace;*
> *foul, I to the Fountain fly;*
> *wash me, Savior, or I die.*[4]

There he was sitting and clothed, which fits in closely with the last trait—he was "in his right mind" (*sophronounta*). It was not a state of mind and manners he brought to himself. It had been accomplished in him by another. He was made right-minded. Jesus, the storm-calming Savior spoke his "Peace! Be still!" as it were, and he brought the man out of his mania into right-mindedness (*sophroneo*)![5] No longer engaging in the unnatural, unrestrained and unrestrainable, nor unsettled and self-destructive—this man had been put in his right mind.

His head was on straight.

He was restfully seated, clothed and covered, and now experiencing real sobriety. We sing:

> *Come, very Sun of heaven's love*
> *in lasting radiance from above,*
> *and pour the Holy Spirit's ray*
> *on all we think or do today.*[6]

This right-minded condition quickly comes out in what the man does next. Mark writes that as Jesus:

> *Was getting into the boat, the man who had been possessed with demons*
> *begged him that he might be with him. And he did not permit him but said*
> *to him, "Go home to your friends and tell them how much the Lord has done*
> *for you, and how he has had mercy on you." And he went away and began*
> *to proclaim in the Decapolis how much Jesus had done for him, and*
> *everyone marveled.* (5:18–20)

The man's sense of community and togetherness was restored. He wanted to be with others, especially his storm-calming Savior. And when Jesus turned him into a different direction, he didn't resume his old ways of self-inflicted solitariness, but he came back into society. He became civil and social.

As I stated at the beginning of the chapter, the whole episode has helped my perception of what it means to be sober-minded. The setting shows a man filled with inner and outer agitation, going and blowing day and night, haunting isolated wastelands, uncivil and hostile in his actions, vocally ranting and raving.

Then the storm-calming Savior, the squall-conquering Sovereign liberates him, and he becomes settled, seated, clothed, covered, serene, and sober!

This is the key to grasping what a life of sobriety looks like, and a picture of what it means to live with our heads on straight. If we have been liberated by our storm-calming Savior, if he has spoken what only he can speak, "Peace! Be still!," and if he has covered over our past disgraces and degenerative habits with all the physical, relational, emotional and psychological scars—then he has given us rest and bestowed freedom from the anxieties and agitations of our hearts and societies. He has handed us a way of living and engaging with others that restores our ability to be civil and social. He has graced us with a whole new opportunity to live life in our right minds.

He is the storm-calming Savior.

Obviously, this doesn't mean there won't be times when we get worried and deeply concerned. I have a friend whose wife was having problems breathing. She went to the doctor and they found a tumor in the lower lobe of her lung. No one can fault him for being concerned and terribly worried. But their trust in the storm-calming Savior carried them through the prognosis and surgery. It is what is holding them up during the painful recovery. Tears were shed, but hope never died. Even the Apostle Paul, who wrote *"Do not be anxious about anything"* (Phil. 4:6a) confessed that *"there is the daily pressure on me of my anxiety for all the churches"* (2 Cor. 11:28). What matters is that the circumstances don't conquer us, but that we come to the storm-calming Savior and trust his "Peace! Be still!"

There was a woman who was nearing the end of her days. I was on my regular hospice in-patient tour, and the nurses informed me that this woman was having the mini seizures that are indications that she was in her final hours. I logged it in my mind and went about my visits.

When I finally got around to her room, I knocked, opened the door, and entered to find her sitting in her chair gazing into the distance. I introduced myself as the hospice chaplain and asked her if she was comfortable and was there anything that was worrying her. She turned to me with a twinkle in her eye and said, "Chaplain, I'm okay, I believe that Jesus died for my sins, and rose again, and that I have nothing to fear about death. But this dying thing is just killing me!"

I almost fell out of my chair with surprise, and together we laughed until tears streamed down our cheeks. We had the sweetest, most joyful fellowship around our common faith in Jesus. She passed away the next day.

This Christian was a woman who was seated, clothed, and in her right mind as she faced our last enemy, death. A sister who had hold of the squall-conquering sovereign God and his "Peace!

Be still!" Here was a believer that will always stand out in my memory as truly sober-minded.

Have you called this storm-calming Savior your Lord? Have you come to believe that he alone makes you clean and right with God? Are you ready to come to him and fall before him? The promises of Scripture are loud and clear for those who come to Jesus. If you:

> Confess with your mouth that Jesus is Lord and believe in your heart that God raised him from the dead, you will be saved. For with the heart one believes and is justified, and with the mouth one confesses and is saved.... For everyone who calls on the name of the Lord will be saved. (Rom. 10:9–10, 13)

Maybe you're someone who has been a Christian for years, but you're racked with anxiety. Perhaps it's distress over your health, your family, your society, or your employment status. Drink in deeply these two stories and let them draw you up close to your storm-calming Savior and cry out to him.

What should you cry? Possibly this will help.

Several years ago, I ran across a short prayer that I have committed to memory. It is one I have used often, even up to the present day. This entreaty repeated below reflects Mark 4:35–5:20 and draws me back to our storm-calming Savior. I encourage you to try it on for size and see if it fits:

> Calm me, O Lord, as You stilled the storm.
> Still me, O Lord, keep me from harm.
> Let all the tumult within me cease.
> Enfold me, Lord, in Your peace.[7]

---

1. Carr, "Dream Deprived: A Modern Epidemic?"
2. Newton 1990 (1779), 460.
3. Crosby 1990 (1875), 605.

4. Toplady 1990 (1776), 499.
5. A similar contrast is made between mania and soberness in Acts 26:25, where Paul is accused of being insane, and retorts that his words are true and sound (*sophrosynes*). Also, in 2 Corinthians 5:13–14, as Paul deals with some thorny issues, he contrasts the charge of have ecstatic visions to being in his right mind (*sophronoumen*).
6. Ambrose 1990 (340–397), 58
7. Northumbria Community, 2019.

AGE, SEX AND STATUS

SOBER-MINDEDNESS IS PERSONAL AND PERVASIVE

Satan, I defy thee;
death, I now decry thee;
fear, I bid thee cease.
World, thou shalt not harm me
nor thy threats alarm me
while I sing of peace.
God's great pow'r guards every hour;
earth and all its depths adore him,
silent bow before him.

—Franck, 1655

He may not be the ideal role model, but his story has a hopeful ring to it. Robert Downey, Jr. was introduced to drugs when he was eight by his father. This blew up into a full-fledged addiction by the time he entered his twenties. His addictions and acting career have swirled around each other for decades. He's been through rehab, relapse, divorce, and arrests.

What brings out hopefulness is that, unlike a few of his movie characters, there is some sense of humility in his perspective. As he mentioned to reporters in 2005:

> I think part of my destiny has to be realizing that I'm not the poster boy for drug abuse, I'm just this guy who has a really strong sense of wanting home and wanting foundation and having not had it, I now choose to create it.[1]

Oddly, I find myself interested in Downey, praying for his continued desire for home and for foundation, keen on his staying "clean" to the very end, and wanting him to flourish.

In a way, Downey's change and turning over a new leaf in life illustrates the way Scripture uses the *sophroneo* words and synonyms. To be sober-minded is not a narrow notion of simply being free from chemical addictions, but more a life of sobriety that affects who we are, how we are, and the way we are. In this chapter we will examine a major scriptural passage that addresses being sober-minded by spending our time in Titus 2. It will become clear that to be sober-minded is personal and pervasive.

Personal

The letter of Paul to his liaison on the Isle of Crete is a short, three-chapter correspondence. Titus has been left on the island by the Apostle to set things in order. Sometime after Paul left, he began receiving reports that there were troublemakers in the churches on Crete who were harming God's people. Therefore, he writes this pastoral letter to enlist Titus' aid in remediating the impact of these agitators. He also seems to be concerned with the societal mores and how the whole community is characterized as being *"liars, evil beasts, lazy gluttons"* (1:12). Therefore, the entire letter is focused on a countercultural approach. It is engrossed with the *"knowledge of the truth, which accords with godliness"* (Titus 1:1c).

Paul is not referring to abstract, theoretical truth, but Gospel truth about who Jesus is and what he has done, is doing, and will do for his people (1:2–3). Further, this truth spawns a godliness that runs along with the Gospel and a lifestyle that concurs with it. This connection plays out in every paragraph from the first to the final words. For example, in the opposite direction, those who are causing trouble *"profess to know God, but they deny him by their works. They are detestable, disobedient, unfit for any good work"* (1:16). Their practice doesn't go along with what they profess. Therefore, Paul motivates Titus to *"teach what accords with sound doctrine"* (2:1), and he immediately starts writing about life-qualities Christians are to exhibit no matter their age, sex, or social standing (2:2–10). This train of reasoning continues to the very end. And it is precisely at chapter 2 that we find out that being sober-minded is personal. It is expected of each age, class and sex of Christians.

Older Men

Older men are to be *"sober-minded, dignified, self-controlled, sound in faith, in love, and in steadfastness"* (2:2). In this verse there are three adjectives ("sober-minded," "dignified," "self-controlled") that are grouped with one participle ("sound") that is driving three nouns ("in faith," in love," and "in steadfastness").

The three adjectives are an emphatic redundancy, stressing what is clearly a serious point to Paul. And these three character-istics are very likely speaking to a peculiar weakness of older men in general but especially on the Isle of Crete. The word translated here, in the ESV, as "sober-minded" is *nephalious*, which can mean simply "to be sober." It regularly shows up in the New Testament teamed together with *sophroneo*, just as it is doing here.

Though it comes straight from the word that means "to be

sober," it bears the thought of "behaving in a sober, restrained manner."[2] The next adjective, "dignified" (*semnous*), has to do with an appropriate, suitable behavior that displays dignity or respect. The last adjective, "self-controlled," is *sophronas*, and it conveys the "good sense" idea. This is that right-mindedness we saw in the previous chapter of this book—a levelheaded and moderate behavior, a sound mind demonstrated in sensible manners.

Taken together, these three adjectives work in unison better than Seal Team Six on a hot mission. Older men are to think soberly, act soberly, and carry themselves soberly. Not only does this caution older men about allowing themselves to be ruled by alcohol, prescription pain medicines, impulse buying, or sexually promiscuous behaviors,[3] but it also encourages them to focus their later years on a life of sobriety, to live a life of clear-headed reasoning and action.

To strengthen this thought, Paul takes these three adjectives and funnels them into the rest of the verse that is being ridden by the participle "sound" ("whole" or "healthy"). The way Paul turns this participle loose on the three following nouns runs together like this: healthy in (the) faith, healthy in (the) love, and healthy in (the) dependable durability. The healthy wholeness of faith, love, and endurance works together with, and works out the lively sobriety of the three adjectives.

For the last two years, I have run one of those four-mile courses that is packed with twenty five obstacles. They call them mud-runs because inevitably, you're caked with muck and mire, sweat, and salt. On several of the obstacles, it is almost impossible to conquer them alone.

One obstacle is the deep mud pit. The walls are slimy, and you need teamwork to get out of that grimy abyss. And so, a person up on the ridge above you puts a hand down, the other behind you gives a shove, and your legs and toes churn their slippery way up the wall.

That's what Paul is doing in Titus 2:2 when he is piling in all these concepts. They are friends working together toward the same end, and that end is having our aged heads on straight. And keep in mind that for older men to be this way—living out these traits—is for them to live along the trail of sound, healthy doctrine. Paul points out: *"But as for you, teach what accords with sound doctrine. Older men are to be…"* (2:1–2a).

It is intriguing that Paul, as an older man himself as he writes these words, heaps it on thick with his fellow older men. But he does so by coming at one idea through several entryways. Though he doesn't get down into specific actions and practices, he lays out a solid principle—sobriety should color and collate our thinking, thriving, living, dying, loving, and leading.

As an older man myself (I'm entering my 60s), delving into this verse and these qualities is quite convicting. But I have also found them helpfully corrective. I am often compelled to ask myself, "Is this action, or attitude, or type of talk, what a sober-minded man is supposed to do or say?"

Next, Paul turns his attention to the older and younger women.

Older and Younger Women

In the subsequent verse, Paul makes a close connection between what he just wrote regarding older men and what he is writing now: "similarly in behavior" (my translation). All that the Apostle has penned for the older men's comportment harmonizes with what he is directing the older women in these following qualities: *"Older women likewise are to be reverent in behavior, not slanderers or slaves to much wine"* (2:3a). In keeping to the right-minded demeanor of verse 2, the older women are to demonstrate a priestly regard for holy things ("reverent in behavior"), which includes not giving into communicating like the devil ("not slanderers" *diabolous*) or giving themselves up to "much wine." Interestingly, Paul doesn't use any of the right-minded words (just yet), but when we recall the "likewise" toward the beginning of the verse it helps us to keep these two sets of characteristics close. Sober-mindedness is implied and begins to come out in the following tasks.

The older women *"are to teach what is good, and so train the young women"* (2:3b–4a). What the older women carry out in life, they are to coach the younger women along the same route. And since Paul has already implied that they are to be sober-minded, he now says they are to "train the young women." In the Greek this directive uses one of the *sophron* words (*sophronizo*), which holds the idea of instructing "someone to behave in a wise and becoming manner"[4] or "train in self-control."[5] Exhibiting good sense, the older women are to sensibly guide the younger women along the same trajectory. And that trajectory includes, *"to love their husbands and children, to be self-controlled* (sophronas), *pure, working at home, kind, and submissive to their own husbands"* (4b–5).

Of all the good qualities and characteristics older women are to sensibly guide younger women with, Paul slips in once more the word translated here as "self-controlled." In its immediate surroundings that quality fills out and includes being discreet as well as sensible (see the NIV, NASB, and RSV).

Without getting lost in the host of heavy and hot debates around 1 Timothy 2:9–15, it is important to note that Paul uses the same word twice. In 1 Timothy 2, Paul explains that *"women should adorn themselves in respectable apparel, with modesty and self-control* (sophrosynes)*"* (2:9). This specifically refers to attire. But then at the end of the paragraph, he attaches the word to both mindset and manners: *"if they continue in faith and love and holiness, with self-control* (sophrosynes)*"* (2:15).

Further, back in Titus 2, Paul points out that the aim for the older women exhibiting good sense and sensibly guiding the younger women along the same sensible trajectory is *"that the word of God may not be reviled"* (5c). This little statement reminds us that Paul is instructing Titus to *"teach what accords with sound doctrine"* (2:1). Older men, older women, and younger women displaying these behaviors then goes along with healthy, whole-some doctrine like a hand in a glove. But what about the younger men?

Younger Men

Titus is not only to rouse the older men and older and younger women toward this goal. In like fashion, he spurs the younger men: *"Likewise, urge the younger men to be self-controlled* (sophronein)" (2:6). I always find Paul's singular injunction to the younger men humorous and likely a shrewd tactic. I am the father of two daughters and two sons, and I have noticed in my thirty four years of parenting that they process "checklists" far differently. My wife and daughters are expert multi-taskers. But I and my sons need to be given only one or two tasks at a time because after that things become a bit cloudy for us.

I'm not certain that's the reason Paul tightens his list down to only one item for younger men, but it fits. And there it is— younger men are to be coached to be *sophroneo*. This word is translated in different versions as "sober-minded," "sensible," or "self-controlled" (NKJV, NIV, NASB). Young men are to be guided toward a right mind and good sense, which is part of what goes along with "sound doctrine" (2:1). But Paul is not done.

Minister and Slaves

If verses 2–6 are not personal enough, the Apostle moves on to two other classes. He addresses his legate, Titus (2:7–8), and Christian slaves (2:9–10). Though he never uses any of the *sophroneo* words in these final verses, the thought is not too far away. Titus is to be a model of good works. His teaching is healthy ("sound speech"), has integrity, and is seemly or "dignified" (*semnoteta*, see v. 2 above). Also, slaves should act in ways that display "good faith" with their masters, and they should be "well-pleasing" (2:9–10).

The aim for both is parallel to the aim for the younger women's actions *"so that an opponent may be put to shame, having nothing evil to say about us"* (2:8) and *"so that in everything they may adorn the doctrine of God our Savior"* (2:10). Even the lifestyle of the minister and the slaves fleshes out "sound doctrine" (2:1).

Why does Paul get so personal with his instructions? For one reason, the Cretans in general are *"always liars, evil beasts, lazy gluttons"* (1:12). That means there is a whole social order that leans in a morally lax direction. Titus is supposed to guide disciples who are all first- and second-generation Christians from Crete, which means they were used to living like "everybody else." They would need help in seeing what a life that is in accord with sound doctrine looks like.

Further, Paul seems to be recruiting the older believers to become mentors and coaches for the younger followers of Jesus in this new way of living. And the troublemakers are slipping into the churches and Christian family gatherings with their insubordinate, empty and deceptive talk (1:10), upsetting whole families to gain wealth (1:11), steering people away from the truth (1:14), and professing to know God, but instead are denying him by their lifestyles (1:16).

Therefore, Paul's directions are antithetical to those mischiefmakers. That's why Paul gets so personal in his instructions on lifestyles that are in "accord with sound doctrine"—a personal approach that spreads out to each age, sex and class.

One of the chief characteristics the Apostle continues to circle back around to is the idea of good sense, being sober-minded, having their heads squarely on their shoulders. In this way, the believers will avoid giving any reason for the Word of God to be reviled (2:5) or providing opponents with fodder for condemning the church's leadership (2:8). He wants the doctrine of God our

Savior to be adorned (2:10). Every man, woman, girl, and boy have a hand in this. Being sober-minded is very personal, which brings Paul to show that it is also pervasive.

Pervasive

After the Apostle has addressed the lifestyle that *"accords with sound doctrine,"* a lifestyle that encompasses each age, sex, and social position (2:1–10), he then comes around to the heart of his directions (2:11–14). That heart is the grace and Gospel *"of our great God and Savior Jesus Christ"* (2:13). But before we jump too far ahead of ourselves, we should see that being sober-minded is exactly what that grace and Gospel cultivate in all Christians.

Grace

With a sudden and surprising shift, the Apostle moves to the appearance of God's grace: *"For the grace of God has appeared, bringing salvation for all people"* (2:11). The "for" points us to the important recognition that the directions of 2:1–10 are because of what Paul is now talking about. In that three-letter word, Paul is saying, "I want you to be this way (2:1–10), and you can because of God's grace (2:11–14)!"

And so, the grace of God has appeared, and it is bringing salvation for "all people." The Apostle has just dealt with every age, sex, and social status in the first ten verses of chapter 2, which colors in what Paul means by "all people." He is saying: "The grace of God has appeared, bringing salvation for all kinds of people, from any class, any age, and sex!"

But why does he bring in grace at this point? It has to do with the next statement.

God's grace is active and instructive. Here's how he put it, *"training us to…, and to…"* (2:12). Grace is God's full-blooded love for us despite what we deserve. It is not placid or passive but has a purpose and point, and it moves us in a specific direction. That direction is away from certain traits and toward other qualities. Therefore, it "trains us." It trains "someone in accordance with proper rules of conduct and behavior."[6] Like a coach, parent, or a tutor, grace guides and mentors us to put away certain habits and take up others. Grace is active and instructive.

On the negative side, grace actively instructs us to *"renounce ungodliness and worldly passions"* (2:12a). In the context of Titus, that especially means to renounce the ungodliness and worldly passions of Cretan society: *"Cretans are always liars, evil beasts, lazy gluttons"* (1:12). But also to renounce the program laid out by the troublemakers (1:13–16). The full-blooded love of God poured out on us despite what we deserve coaches and leads us to put away and turn away from all allegiance to and acceptance of the social mores that promote ungodliness and worldly passions— those ways of living, loving, voting, shopping, parenting, and playing that turn their backs instead of their faces to God (Jer. 2:27).

But positively, the full-blooded love of God poured out on us despite what we deserve also leads us to take up a new approach *"and to live self-controlled* (sophronos), *upright, and godly lives in the present age"* (2:12b). These three adverbs are qualities that result from God's gracious training and guiding. The first is *sophronos* which is translated variously, such as self-control, soberly, sensibly, and sober (ESV and NIV, KJV and NKJV, NASB, RSV). Since verse 1, this word has been the consistent trait to be exercised by older men and women and younger women and men. Further, the company the word keeps in this verse shows that it is more than a mental or rational virtue. It is a way of living, "to live self- controlled/soberly" right along with righteousness ("up-right"—*dikaios*) and godliness (*eusebos*). To live soberly is to live in a manner that goes well with righteousness and godliness. Lastly, it is achievable "in this present age." The grace of God fashions us to experience growing in wholesome right-minded ways in the here-and-now as we move toward the there-and-then.

Gospel

The there-and-then is hugely important for the here-and-now, as Paul shows: *"waiting for our blessed hope, the appearing of the glory of our great God and Savior Jesus Christ"* (2:13). These living, grace- guided qualities of being sober-minded, righteous, and godly are how we live in this present age (the here-and-now) as we actively wait and eagerly anticipate with open arms the return of our *"our great God and Savior Jesus Christ"* (the there-and-then)!

This active waiting and eager anticipation remind me of that time when I had ordered a new laptop. I was excited that I could finally afford a new one, and I had been notified it was coming that day by a delivery service.

It affected the whole day for me. I tried to distract myself by doing other tasks around the house. But every time a big truck would rumble down the road, I would jump up and run out the door to see where that truck was. I would strain my neck looking this way and then that. I spent time clearing away space for it and making sure I had a place to unpack it to explore its programs. My expectancy modified the way I spent the whole morning into the early afternoon.

Finally, the moment came and up rolled the big, brown delivery van, and I was out the door beaming from ear-to-ear. I'm sure I must have looked like a little boy getting a Christmas present! That's the kind of eager anticipation we have for the there-and-then that affects how we live in the here-and-now.

But why does the there-and-then have so much to do with our here-and-now? Because of what our great God and Savior Jesus Christ has done way-back-when. As the Apostle goes on to say: *"Who gave himself for us to redeem us from all lawlessness and to purify for himself a people for his own possession who are zealous for good works"* (2:14).

This great God and Savior—who is the grace of God in the flesh—gave himself to liberate and emancipate us from *"ungodliness and worldly passions"* (2:12a), those old ways of lawlessness. He gave himself to set us on a new path, to move us along a new course of living soberly, righteously and godly in this present age (2:12b), *"and to purify for himself a people for his own possession who are zealous for good works"* (2:14b). Notice, then, how the grace and Gospel of our great God and Savior changes everything about us.

That's what Paul is hammering home for these Christians on Crete. Once they were just like their culture and community— liars, gluttons and evil beasts (1:12)—but now they have been released and renewed to live a life of sobriety.

Because of the grace and Gospel of our great God and Savior Jesus Christ, then older men, older women, younger women, younger men, ministers, and slaves can embody a whole new way of being human.

It's a way that exhibits having our heads on straight!

Therefore, not only is having a sober-mind personal (getting down into each age group, sex, and social status). It is pervasive (all those whom Jesus has emancipated).

To be sober-minded is an important and expected trait. Our growing desire to become more and more settled in mind and conduct is part-and-parcel of the grace and Gospel of Jesus Christ.

We have begun to tap into some of the different aspects of what it means to be sober-minded, and Titus 2 is a big help in that regard. It would be worth your time to slowly go back through what we have just spent several pages developing and classify what you've learned. Then, as a further benefit, take those characteristics and turn them into prayer. For example, if you're an older man, spend time in 2:2 and beseech the Lord of 2:11–14 to fortify and bolster you in being sober-minded, dignified, and self-controlled as you grow healthier in faith, love, and steadfast endurance.

As you move through your day, remember what the grace and Gospel of our great God and Savior has liberated you to do and be and find ways to put it into practice.

But is there more to being sober-minded?

Are there other aspects of how it looks and the way it perceives circumstances?

Does being sober-minded impact our relationships in and out of the church?

The next chapter will begin to examine these possibilities.

---

1. Biography, "Robert Downey Jr."
2. Louw and Nida, "Semantic Domains."
3. The rise of sexually transmitted disease among middle age and senior men is on the rise in North America. See Harvard Health Letter, "Sexually transmitted disease? At my age?"
4. Louw and Nida, Op. Cit.
5. Zerwick and Grosvenor, *Grammatical Analysis of Greek New Testament*, 649.
6. Louw and Nida, Op. Cit.

SOBER JUDGMENT

OUR RESPONSE TO GOD'S MERCY

SOVEREIGN COMMANDER OF THE UNIVERSE,
I am sadly harassed by doubts, fears, unbelief,
in a felt spiritual darkness.
My heart is full of evil surmisings and disquietude,
and I cannot act faith at all...
Help me, O Lord, to throw myself absolutely
and wholly on thee, for better, for worse, without comfort....
All-wise God, Thy never-failing providence
orders every event, sweetens every fear,
reveals evil's presence lurking in seeming good,
brings real good out of seeming evil,
makes unsatisfactory what I set my heart upon,
to show me what a short-sighted creature I am,
and to teach me to live by faith upon
thy blessed self....

—Arthur Bennet, *Valley of Vision*

I once served a congregation in a totally different space-and-time continuum from where I am now. It was divided into two clans.

There was the "in-town" extended family and the "outlanders." The tensions in that church were stark. After every Sunday service ended, they would all vacate the church and leave it a ghost land within five minutes. The dislikes and disagreements had piled up over three or four generations, and they couldn't be in the same room looking and talking to each other for more than a few seconds.

But there was one moment every year when everything changed, when there was a sparkle of hope. Right after the Christmas Eve service, they would talk to each other, smile, enjoy catching up, and spread good cheer.

It was like they had all come into their right mind for one night. That annual scene of harmony and healthiness should have been the normal, weekly experience, and what we are getting into in this chapter speaks to this.

I recently took our congregation through Romans 12. It was instructive, corrective, and eye-opening. The first few verses are so familiar that they can easily flow right past and slide on by with quaint Christianese.

To begin, chapter 12 is a new section in Paul's letter. Chapters 1–11 have tackled the realization that every people-group—Jews, Gentiles, Romans and Greeks—are all in sin and under its curse. But, in his faithfulness to himself and his promise to Abraham, God has graciously brought forth the remedy to humankind's condition, and it is found in Jesus Christ. If we rely on our do-good-ism, law keeping, and so on, then we find that we remain condemned. But if we believe in our hearts that God raised Jesus from the dead and confess him as Lord, we will discover that Jesus died for our sins and was raised for our justification.

Whether we are Jews or Gentiles, this is how God has given

us hope and how he manifests costly love: *"God shows his love for us in that while we were still sinners, Christ died for us"* (5:8). Then comes chapter 12: *"I appeal to you therefore, brothers, by the mercies of God"* (12:1a).

Paul is saying, "I entreat you that because of God's rich mercies and grace, which I've just spent eleven chapters unpacking, that you respond this way!" The response has three basic parts that are interrelated.

Responses

Our initial response is to offer ourselves up to God like the priestly clan from the Old Testament, the Levites *"to present your bodies as a living sacrifice, holy and acceptable to God, which is your spiritual worship"* (12:1b). The Levites were living sacrifices in their service to God, as is noted several times in Numbers 8. For example, *"And Aaron shall offer the Levites before the LORD as a wave offering from the people of Israel, that they may do the service of the LORD"* (Num. 8:11).

It was not a life-threatening, blood-letting sacrifice but a life of service and commitment to Yahweh and his people. Offering ourselves in this way and with this understanding is our "spiritual worship" or more literally, or our reasonable service. God's people are a priestly people, offered up to God to serve him.

Further, we are to turn from one way of seeing life and circumstances toward a new way: *"Do not be conformed to this world, but be transformed by the renewal of your mind"* (12:2a). Because of God's full-blooded love poured out on us despite what we deserve (chapters 1–11) we come around to a new way of reasoning, thinking, loving and living. The aim is so *"that by testing you may discern what is the will of God, what is good and acceptable and perfect"* (12:2b).

By taking on a better way of perceiving and proceeding, we grow in grasping God's will—which is good, acceptable, and perfect—in the midst of a murky, mussed-up world where things can be confused and cloudy. Priests distinguish between the common and holy, the clean and unclean, for the sake of God's honor and for the good of others.

Then Paul gets a little closer to where we sit in the pew. The third behavioral change with which we should respond to the rich mercy of God comes down to our main subject:

> For by the grace given to me I say to everyone among you not to think of himself more highly than he ought to think, but to think with sober judgment (sophronein), each according to the measure of faith that God has assigned. (13:3)

Since God has been so mercifully lavish toward us (Rom. 1-11), we should give ourselves in priestly ways as living sacrifices, which is proper for priests (12:1). That means we turn away from reasoning and reacting in the ways our society does as those who have never known or reveled in the mercy of God in Christ. We're to take up a God-renewed mind that better comprehends the ways of God (12:2).

This brings us to the more pointed point of verse three. "For" alerts us to the inner connection of this third verse with the previous two and says "Because" or "For this reason." To paraphrase, Paul is saying:

> Because of verses 1-2, I say to all of you—I say it by the grace given to me—don't be high-minded and haughty in your self-awareness and self-perception, your assertions and assessments, but rather, be like the stormy soul liberated by the storm-calming Savior. Be seated, clothed and in your right mind, trusting as God has enabled you to trust.

In this passage the opposite of high-minded thinking is sober judgment. This is a way of being self-aware and sensibly adjusted that sees faith as wholly God's gift and not a result of personally superior powers, or cognitive prowess. Therefore, sober judgment or sobriety clearly carries the idea of humility, the kind of humility that impacts our relationships. One author writes, "God's grace in the gospel creates a gospel-wrought humility, which in turn, leads to a gospel-driven unity."[1] Further, where Paul's "think with sober judgment" sits in Romans 12, we can better grasp the relational aspects Paul meant by this phrase.

Relationships

What are some of the social characteristics shaped by thinking with this sober judgment? Paul begins the next verse with a "For as," notifying us to various ways sober judgment acts and associates. He writes:

> For as in one body we have many members, and the members do not all have the same function, so we, though many, are one body in Christ, and individually members one of another. (12:4–5)

Sober judgment recognizes what it means to be connected to other "body parts" and becomes better at functioning well on a team. It has a growing situational awareness that picks up relational nuances and interpersonal objectives for the goal of a congregation's health and wellbeing. It has a grace-filled self-awareness that sees that it must engage with other believers using the gifts it has received for the benefit of the whole and the members of the whole (12:6–8). In this way, sober judgment helps to foster fellowship, communal faith, and healthiness. In the words of one author, "The flame of individual faith weakens when it is alone, but in true community the fire of faith illumines the night."[2] Maybe it's coincidental, but the stormy soul in Mark 5 is anti-social, running away from community. But when the Squall- conquering Sovereign rescued him, part of his being in his right mind (*sophronounta*) was that he was restored to his community. Sober judgment (*sophronein*) leads us to engage with God's community in fitting ways.

Additionally, as Paul charges forward in Romans 12, he launches into a series of short, rapid-fire injunctions. These directives address in greater detail how a sober-minded perspective interlocks with others inside the church (12:9–13). It is having the good sense to love and love well (9a, 10a, 13), to be humble and never haughty (10), to hate what is evil and act like one married to good (9b), and to stick to your trust in the Lord (11–12). A life of sober judgment takes on the responsibility of interacting internally with God's people in wholesome ways and with healthy words.

This is an important awareness to have in our age, where people wish to claim to be followers of Jesus but want nothing to do with being involved in a fellowship of Jesus' people. My question for them is—are they really following Jesus in his grace-given sober judgment way, or are they being conformed to the life-patterns of our American world with its intense rugged individualism?

Peter presents a similar point, though in a shorter fashion. He places together two words that carry the idea of being sober, and leads off with them:

> *The end of all things is at hand; therefore be self-controlled* (sophroneo) *and sober-minded* (napho) *for the sake of your prayers. Above all, keep loving one another earnestly, since love covers a multitude of sins. Show hospitality to one another without grumbling. As each has received a gift, use it to serve one another, as good stewards of God's varied grace: whoever speaks, as one who speaks oracles of God; whoever serves, as one who serves by the strength that God supplies—in order that in everything God may be glorified through Jesus Christ. To him belong glory and dominion forever and ever. Amen.* (1 Peter 4:7–11)

In the words of one commentator, Peter presses home that the Christian community must not:

> Give way to eschatological frenzy in face of the imminent end of things. To do so is to fall victim to the world. The required moderation is sustained by faith and issues in prayer and love (v. 8). More than the philosophical attitude is thus at issue.[3]

In the above passage, Peter uses the two "sober" words to nail together the significant value of not only having our heads on straight but that we are to have good sense in our involvement with each other, along with the use of the gifts we have received, for the betterment of one another.

No matter the shortness of our moment in history, whether it's the looming destruction of Jerusalem, the end of history as we know it, or the final coming of Jesus, we're to have our heads on straight, serving one another soundly and sympathetically. But not only does sober judgment impact our relations inside the church, it enables us to deal more wholesomely with even messier conditions.

Retaliation

Paul charges on in Romans 12 to point out that this sober judgment is having the good sense to respond to evil rightly, whether that evil arises from inside or outside of a given congregation (12:14–21). Paul mixes together the multiple directives in this paragraph, and it quickly becomes obvious that he sees (and has experienced) evil raising its grisly head from within churches as well as from the outside community.

And so, his instructions help us to remain on our feet and not get swept away when we see the nasty and nauseous coming at us from Christians or non-Christians. Original sin (and total depravity for that matter) doesn't stop at the church door and get left in the umbrella stand in the foyer.

Therefore, this grace-fortified-sober-mind perspective fleshes out in actions of empathy (14–15), humility (16, see v.3 and 10), intentional thoughtfulness on ways to do what is honorable in dishonorable circumstances (17), the growing awareness that recognizes our limitations in fostering peace (18), and the good sense to see that it's not our domain to dole out vengeance.

Consequently, in taking up this sober judgment, we are not to be *"overcome by evil, but overcome evil with good"* (19–21). We are not to be conquered and vanquished by the malevolent.

We conquer it. We gain victory over it (Greek: *nikao*) through temperate and prudent actions.

This rich mine of mandates is worth digging deeper into, and there are helpful resources toward that end. For example, Jay Adams's book *Overcoming Evil* carefully teases out many of the qualities in 12:14–21. But for now, it is enough to come to grips with the realization that living soberly does not get swallowed up in retaliation.

I think the perspective of 12:1–21 is clear—sober judgment affects our interactions within the messiness of being the multi-membered body of Christ. But it also tempers our reactions to the scrappy and scruffy tumble, whether communally or congregationally. This aids us to not become consumed by malevolence but to overcome it by good.

If one allows Paul's "think with sober judgment" to have its way with them, they will find the concept guiding Christians' actions and relationships all the way to Romans 15:13. Instead of doling out vengeance, we leave place to the wrath of God (12:19), and now have the good sense to see that one way God uses to bring his vengeance is through the civil magistrate, who is *"God's servant for your good… an avenger who carries out God's wrath on the wrongdoer"* (13:4).

Obviously, not every magistrate or government is as

concerned with justice as we would like. The authorities and administration in Paul's day weren't. Thus, we don't allow ourselves to become swept up into the swirling euphoria of utopian political promises and programs that assure us they will usher in the Kingdom of God or Shangri La if you will only vote or promote their agenda. Nor do we side with those movements and measures that desire to throw off the regime to create its own justice. Part of sober judgment considers that justice now is, at best, marginal. But our ultimate allegiance and expectation is both that God can, and many times does, bring about just resolutions in the here-and-now; but he will finally, and surely, right all wrongs in the return of his Son.

When I posted on a social media site that I was writing this book, I received several positive responses. One of them sticks out.

An older friend of mine wrote:

> I will buy this book. It needs to be written. I'm not the expert, but I'll say this much–the reading I've been required to do for a class I'm taking at college this semester, "Augustine and His Legacy," has caused me to repent of the idolatry of touting one political group and its solutions over another and of the worse sin of letting these allegiances leak into my approaches to what's going on "in the church." All of the utopias being peddled in the earthly city are destined to fail, and allowing any party into the church is setting it up for failure, too. My problem now is that, with the smashing of so many idols, I'm standing amidst the ruin of my politics and trying to figure out how my renewed life in Christ begins. I hope your book goes somewhere I need to.[4]

This is the uncomfortable bench we sit and squirm about on.

Having sober judgment and living soberly will likely ensure we feel this tension until our death or the day when Jesus returns to judge the living and the dead.

Yet, being sober-minded has no room for *acedia*—that is, sloth and despondency. Though this book is not delving into the classic virtue studies, it is helpful to take note that temperance (the normal translation of Aristotle's use of *sophrosyne*) does not preclude anger. Rather, temperance and sobriety have space for anger, but it must be in accord with reason and in opposition to evil.[5]

Or better still, in quoting Psalm 4:4 and 37:8, Paul instructs Christ's people, *"Be angry and do not sin; do not let the sun go down on your anger, and give no opportunity to the devil"* (Eph. 4:26–27). Sober judgment opens out to faith that God cares about this injustice or that wickedness and allows the civil magistrate to be God's diaconal instrument. And, at times, sober judgment will see the need to nudge or help the magistrate to take just actions.

But if, and when, the civil realm falls into crookedness, crony-ism, clumsiness, or carelessness, we keep our heads on straight, remembering who it is that calms the storm and conquers the squall, and we place our ultimate and utmost reliance there. But then, there is more.

Paul goes on to write that our task is to exhibit love (13:8–10). This love is never lawless, but it is always lawful. Though I have read and heard many teachers and writers take 13:8–10 to mean that love is other than or distinct from God's law, Paul is showing here that true love is always lawful and never lawless, *"for the commandments are summed up in this word, 'You shall love your neighbor as yourself'"* (13:9).

Paul doesn't say the commandments are sidelined by this love. Nor does he say the commandments are done away by this love. Quite clearly his point is that, if you love, it will look like the Ten Commandments.

If you love, you won't steal but will promote the safety of other folks' property. If you love, you won't take another person's spouse but will promote their marital integrity. If you love you won't murder, taking life unjustly, but you will uphold life. To live with sober judgment is to live by lawful love.

But also notice that right after Paul remarked on the civil magistrate, he mentions that the gauge of love is not what the magistrate dictates but what God has prescribed. As someone once said to me many years ago, "What's legal is not always lawful. And what's lawful is not always legal." This friend's point was that the laws of the city of man may at times be at cross purposes with the law of the city of God.

Love, then, is lawful as God has defined lawfulness. There are times, therefore, when sober judgment dictates that when the regime is not being what God calls it to be, we may need to quietly continue to do what is right in God's eyes, as defined most precisely in sacred Scripture.

To lawfully love as God defines it is not about grandstanding, body-counts, virtue-signaling, or attention getting. Rather, lawful love pursues what God has clarified regarding the common good. And we do so by remembering that "the night is far gone; the day is at hand."

Thus we "walk properly as in the daytime," putting off old ways and putting on the Lord Jesus Christ, making "no provision for the flesh, to gratify its desires" (13:11–14).[6]

These last words fit in with Paul's *sophronein*, sober judgment, which is very much about having the good sense to not allow our desires and passions to rule us. Therefore, instead of giving in to our predilections, penchants, and proclivities, we soberly and steadfastly give in to Jesus the storm-calming Savior. This, then, takes us deeper into our personal relationships, especially within the Christ-community.

Rifts and Regrets

Paul shows how our relationships in the congregation between differing levels of "strong" and "weak in the faith" follows the

Gospel way of fostering unity and humility, so that we care for and about each other. Since none of us lives or dies to himself; and since *"to this end Christ died and lived again, that he might be Lord both of the dead and of the living"* (14:9); and since *"Christ did not please himself, but as it is written, 'The reproaches of those who reproached you fell on me'"* (15:3); and since we must all stand before the judgment seat of God to give account of our actions (14:10–12); then let us have the sobriety and good sense to *"pursue what makes for peace and for mutual upbuilding"* (14:9).

As Christopher Hutchinson observes, humility:

> Toward one another is the missing link between grace and unity, and it is the glue that holds" us "together....What is needed to bring truth and love, and grace and unity together is a deep and growing humility stemming from the Gospel. Believers must walk with one another in gentleness and patience. They must bear with one another in love. True unity takes more than good intention or doctrinal agreement or hard work. It takes gospel-wrought humility.[7]

It is apparent that Paul's point is that the living-sacrifice-transformed-mind-sober-judgement way (12:1–3) that explodes from God's gracious gift in Christ (chapters 1–11), impacts and affects not only our cognitive faculties alone but our relational engagements with all of our words and ways.

As stated earlier, humility goes along with sobriety, so Hutchinson has hit the nail squarely on the head. Sober judgment, therefore, is deeply concerned with rifts and regrets in God's church, and it works away from them toward a wholesome welcoming: *"Therefore welcome one another as Christ has welcomed you, for the glory of God"* (15:7).

All of this begins with the mercy of God (12:1–3) and requires the ongoing work of God. How fitting, then, that we should add our voices to Paul's and pray for ourselves and one another: *"May the God of hope fill you with all joy and peace in believing, so that by the power of the Holy Spirit you may abound in hope"* (15:13).

Review

From this short excursion into Romans 12:1–15:13, we get a healthy sense of what it looks like to be sober-minded. Let's review by way of a series of bullet points:

- A sober life gushes out of the Gospel (Romans chapters 1–11)—*"I appeal to you therefore, bothers, by the mercies of God"* (12:1).
- It comes from our Gospel-made priesthood as living sacrifices (12:1).
- And it arises out of our transformed and renewed mindedness (12:2).
- Instead of thinking more highly of ourselves than we ought, we follow through with sober judgment (12:3).
- Which means we see our role in bettering God's congregation and building up God's people (12:4–8).
- Further, having sober judgment leads us in our relationships inside the church (12:9–13).
- It enables us to steadily and sturdily face evil, no matter where it comes from, not with vengeance but victory (12:14–21).
- With sober judgment, we step back from vengefulness and retaliation and give place to God's ordinary and orderly way of righting wrongs, one of which is the civil magistrate (13:1–7).
- And living soberly means loving with lawful love (13:8–10) facing toward the coming of Jesus (13:11–14).
- Finally, it gets down into the dirty details of the often messiness of congregational life, especially where

conflicting ideas and idiosyncrasies regularly create rifts and regrets (14:1–15:13).

---

1. Christopher Hutchinson, *Rediscovering Humility*, 180.
2. Kelly Kapic, *Embodied Hope*, 126–7.
3. Bromiley 1985, 1044.
4. This statement is taken from a response to my Facebook post on 10 October 2019. It is used by permission from the author, John McNeely Hudson.
5. For more on this, see Josef Pieper's *The Four Cardinal Virtues*, p. 193–197; and Zac Cogley's "A Study of Virtuous and Vicious Anger" in *Virtues & Their Vices*, ed. by Kevin Tempe and Craig A. Boyd. Both volumes have chapters on the role of anger within the virtue of temperance.
6. It was these very verses that God used to convert Augustine as he heard the children's voices tauntingly say, "tolle lege, take up and read".
7. Op Cit., 177.

GOD'S HAND ON GOD'S MAN

No guilt in life, no fear in death,
This is the power of Christ in me
From life's first cry to final breath,
Jesus commands my destiny
No power of hell, no scheme of man,
Can ever pluck me from His hand
Till He returns or calls me home
Here in the power of Christ I'll stand.

—Keith Getty and Stuart Townsend, 2002

It was nearing the winter of 1890–91. Wooden Lance and the other Kiowas were hearing from the Cheyenne and Arapaho about the Man from the North and his visions. He was supposed to have seen Jesus, and the country where their dead ones now lived, a place also filled with buffalo. It was a vision of the land before white settlers and soldiers had changed everything. The vision led the Man from the North to say that they were to run off the white people. Then, the land would be restored to them, their dead would come back, and the buffalo would return. Attending the visions was the Ghost Dance that stirred up hopes but also whipped up high expectations for a fight. Wooden Lance began to wonder if this all could be possible.

Wooden Lance had been disillusioned from another "new" ceremony four years earlier. It was known as "the buffalo coming out ceremony." He really wanted this new thing to be true because he had recently lost his little daughter and missed her deeply. But instead of getting swept up into the frenzy of the moment, he headed out to find the Man of the North and investigate this new ceremony and the visions on his own.

He travelled from tribe to tribe, riding horses and even a train, until he landed way up north. Finally, gaining help from the Shoshoni, he was led to the Paiutes. There he was introduced to the Man of the North. Wooden Lance informed the man why he was there and began to ask him questions. The man recounted how his dances took him out of this world into a heavenly land of flowers, the place with each of his loved ones who were now gone. There, in that visionary land, they told him how happy they were there, but that they would be even happier to come back. The man understood that the white people needed to be removed from the land so that there would be space for the dead ones to return.

At this point Wooden Lance simply asked, "Why are you the one to know these things? Why are you the one that's teaching this belief? Why does this come to one man and not to some other?"

In response, the man related how he was orphaned, and the whites brought him up. They taught him about Jesus, the only thing he thought was good. Once he grew up, he ran away but took the Jesus teaching with him. It was then he began to think—if God had one son he could also have more. Then it came to him that he was the other son of God, and that's how he knew his visions were true and certain.

Wooden Lance left, carrying his thoughts with him. He understood that the Man from the North was simply a normal man and was one who didn't live what he taught, therefore "what he believed couldn't be true. Wooden Lance had to hurry, hurry, and tell the Kiowas what wasn't true."[1]

Wooden Lance wanted what he had heard to be true. He strongly yearned to hold his dead daughter again. Yet he had the good sense to think and ask and not get caught up in the emotional swirl around him. Wooden Lance illustrates another aspect of what it means to be sober-minded.

Up to this point, we have worked our way through three major sections of Scripture that have led us in what it means to be sober-minded (*sophroneo*). There was the stormy soul in Mark 5:1–20, to whom Jesus' "Peace! Be still!" brought him to be sitting, clothed and in his right mind. Then we examined how Paul wanted Titus to promote what was proper for sound doctrine in Titus 2:1–14, and were met by the role of sober living for each age, status and sex; and that it is one of the traits grace teaches Christ's expectant, redeemed people. Last, there was Romans 12:1–15:13 and the function of sober judgment as part of our Gospel-wrought priesthood and renewed mind that impacted our words and ways inside the congregation as well as outside.

In each of these biblical studies, it is evident that to be sober-minded is cognitive, but it also has much to do with growing in good sense, not caught up in panic but pushing on in fidelity, fraternity, and faith. Which leads us to consider a circumstance in the Hebrew scriptures that fits into one aspect of a sober life—having the right kind of fear.

God's Hand

Isaiah was God's spokesperson to his people during some rough and raucous days. Times went from decent to bad to better to hair-raisingly scary!

During a particularly dreadful season under the reign of Ahaz, God spoke a highly poignant word to Isaiah. Ahaz was engaged in a social campaign to synchronize God's ways and worship with the dominant culture around him. He was losing hold on his national turf, and he was losing his nerve, so he was grasping at Syrian straws to shore up his security (Isa. 7:1–9 and 2 Kings 16). His compromises and moral collapses earned him this epitaph:

> He did not do what was right in the eyes of the LORD his God, as his father David had done, but he walked in the way of the kings of Israel... according to the despicable practices of the nations whom the LORD drove out before the people of Israel. (2 Kings 16:2–3)

The king also pulled into his religious orbit a complicit priest, Uriah, who would further his latitudinarian liberalizing. And so, because of the persistent faith-breaking of Ahaz, God announces the coming of a conquering foe.

In the midst of this dire season of worry and fear (Isa. 8:1–10), God speaks a sobering word to Isaiah. It is a word of assurance (8:11–13) that is surrounded by judgment (8:14–15), warning (8:16–22), and hope (9:1–7). Our focus in this chapter is on the message of assurance in 8:11–13:

> For the LORD spoke thus to me with his strong hand upon me, and warned me not to walk in the way of this people, saying: "Do not call conspiracy all that this people calls conspiracy, and do not fear what they fear, nor be in dread. But the LORD of hosts, him you shall honor as holy. Let him be your fear, and let him be your dread.

To unpack these verses, we will look at God's assuring hand, his assuring correction, and finally his assuring dread.

God's Assuring Hand

The description is both comforting and calming. God's hand being on his people is normally a good thing in Scripture, though at times it is discomfiting.

Elymas the magician found out what it was to have the hand of the Lord upon him to restrain him from making crooked the straight paths of the Lord (Acts 13:9–11). And the psalmist sang about God's hand being heavy on him while he tried to hide his sin until he came to confess his wrongs and obtained release (Ps. 32:4).

Yet, more often than not, to have the hand of the Lord resting on someone was fortifying and comforting. Such as when the believers fled Jerusalem and arrived in Antioch declaring the good news of the Lord Jesus and found *"the hand of the Lord was with them,"* which resulted in *"a great number who believed"* turning to the Lord (Acts 11:21).

Or when Ezra and Nehemiah returned to tumbled-down Jerusalem (Ezra 7:9, 28; 8:18, 31; Neh. 2:8, 18) to restore the city and worship in God's temple. The comforting and fortifying hand of God on a person is the experience of God's people when they need help to keep the faith (Ps. 73:23–26); and when his people need strength to trust in desperate times (1 Pet. 5:6–11). And so, it is fitting that as Isaiah's society was sliding into social mayhem and the governmental administration was legislating synchronizing God's ways and worship with the dominant cultural mores, that *"the LORD spoke thus to me with his strong hand upon me."* With God's assuring hand on Isaiah came God's assuring correction.

God's Assuring Correction

God's assuring hand on the prophet was undoubtedly meant to comfort and fortify, but it was also correcting. We read: *"and warned me not to walk in the way of this people."* Very much like the sober judgment approach in Romans 12, God's assuring hand encourages Isaiah to not:

> Be conformed to this world, but be transformed by the renewal of your mind, that by testing you may discern what is the will of God, what is good and acceptable and perfect. (Rom. 12:2)

The "way of the world" around Isaiah was Ahaz's synchronizing policy coupled with the fear of a coming calamity. In that environment, the social pressure can push in hard, constricting and choking life out of a soul. And God's assuring hand pulls Isaiah up to fresh air, opening to him a new way of perceiving his age and era.

The southern Catholic writer, Flannery O'Connor, once wrote:

> Push back against the age as hard as it pushes against you. What people don't realize is how much religion costs. They think faith is a big electric blanket, when of course it is the cross.[2]

Similarly, the Apostle Paul instructs us to look:

> Carefully then how you walk, not as unwise but as wise, making the best use of the time, because the days are evil. Therefore do not be foolish, but understand what the will of the Lord is. (Eph. 5:15–17)

God's assuring hand is a correcting hand, fortifying and comforting his people. It raises us up out of the suffocating social synchronization, fear, and fuss. It allows us to fill our lungs with fresh air. And the make-up of this fresh air is likely to shock us because it comes from God's assuring dread.

God's Assuring Dread

God's assuring hand corrects the prophet in a surprising way that fortifies him in his environment. God's hand on Isaiah warns him not to walk in the way of this people, and is clarified with these words:

> *Do not call conspiracy all that this people calls conspiracy, and do not fear what they fear, nor be in dread. But the LORD of hosts, him you shall honor as holy. Let him be your fear, and let him be your dread.* (Isa. 8:12–14)

To have God as our dread frees us up from the dreadful panic and conspiracies of a community going whacky. The alternative is explained by Os Guinness. He writes, "Those who *perceive* themselves as victims and respond by *portraying* themselves as victims end by *paralyzing* themselves as victims."[3] Either we thrive in the fear of God or sink in paralyzing panic.

When one of my friends, Stephanie Chen, read that last paragraph and especially the final sentence, she made a telling observation. She said:

> If I'm hiking, I can be scared of bugs, thorns, and poison ivy, but the second a bear shows up I'm scared of nothing but that! The object we fear re-prioritizes everything around it.

Either we thrive in the fear of God or sink in paralyzing panic. Marilynne Robinson, the Pulitzer Prize-winning author of *Gilead*, penned an essay on fear a few years back. Whether one agrees with her view of gun control or not, the treatise is worth a thoughtful read on several levels. In that piece she wisely notes that:

First, contemporary America is full of fear. And second, fear is not a Christian habit of mind... Christ is a gracious, abiding presence in all reality, and in him history will finally be resolved.[4]

It seems to me Robinson is on to something here. She goes on further to state:

Granting the perils of the world, it is potentially a very costly indulgence to fear indiscriminately, and to try to stimulate fear in others, just for the excitement of it, or because to do so channels anxiety or loneliness or prejudice or resentment into an emotion that can seem to those who indulge it like shrewdness or courage or patriotism. But no one seems to have an unkind word to say about fear these days, un-Christian as it surely is.[5]

To live in fear and to stimulate fear in others.

Yahweh tells Isaiah and us that it's better to have God as our liberating dread. This is the God who became human for us and our salvation. He triumphed over the world, the flesh and the Devil in his death, resurrection, and ascension. He will one day return to judge both the living and the dead. But to fear evil more than God is—to put it biblically and pointedly—to become worshippers of evil. Fear and worship go hand in glove in sacred Scripture. Of all people on this round globe, we have nothing to fear, and we have been told so hundreds of times in Holy Writ, "Fear not!" A sober-minded people know whom to fear and whom not to.

Many years ago in the 1980s, I became friends with a group of people in south central Texas who were convinced that there was a massive conspiracy to destroy the United States of America. By their talk, it sometimes seemed that the conspiracy morphed into a conglomeration of several conspiracies. Their fear became contagious. I started feeling afraid too. Their dread became my dread.

For example, one time they were convinced that a particular Communist country had several mechanized battalions (tanks and troops) amassing on the Mexican side of the border. They talked about the numerous eyewitnesses who had seen them and were reporting to a select number of people in the US. This went on for weeks.

As the days rolled on, my friends would recount how long it would take the units to cross the border and show up on our doorsteps and the hopeless situation we were in. It was unnerving to talk with them. The atmosphere was infectious, and I nearly succumbed to their panic.

I started planning exit strategies, even spending a few restless nights having nightmares. Then, in a fleeting moment of thoughtfulness like Wooden Lance mentioned at the beginning of this chapter, I started asking questions.

Mainly, I asked them for proof. Surely, they could jimmy up some photographs or footage that we could examine. Instead, there was silence. As I pressed harder, there was only hemming and hawing. Finally, after my persistent demand for some tangible verification beyond the hearsay, they acknowledged they had nothing.

As I left them, it dawned on me that I had been duped by their panic. But what truly struck me was how I had let myself do the unthinkable—I momentarily stepped away from trusting in God's faithfulness and sovereign control. I feared their fear and dreaded their dread.

But even if what these friends said was true, the God of Abraham, Isaac, and Jacob was greater and mightier, and he could be relied on no matter what happened. The One who can topple Egyptian armies in red seas, as well as turn proud Babylonian Emperors into babbling buffoons is the One to fear. The One who could read through Ananias's and Saphira's deceitful hearts and words, and thus send them to an early grave, is the One to dread. Even our Lord pointedly stated: *"And do not fear those who kill the body but cannot kill the soul. Rather fear him who can destroy both soul and body in hell"* (Matt. 10:28).

What was I doing but fearing evil more than fearing God, the God whose fear is surrounded by his mercy and grace! That's how he described himself after bringing discipline on, and restoration to, his bull-worshipping people:

> *The LORD, the LORD, a God merciful and gracious, slow to anger, and abounding in steadfast love and faithfulness, keeping steadfast love for thousands, forgiving iniquity and transgression and sin, but who will by no means clear the guilty, visiting the iniquity of the fathers on the children and the children's children, to the third and the fourth generation.* (Exod. 34:6–7)

The relationship of justice and grace are brought out by Carmen Joy Imes when she writes, "God's grace coexists with his justice. They are both integral to his character."[6] Thus, when the redeeming, rescuing Yahweh is our dread and fear, we can be settled and in our right minds, no longer calling conspiracy what the people call conspiracy, fearing what they fear, or walking about in dread.

Why? Because the storm-calming Savior and squall-conquering Sovereign has this! God's assuring dread is sobering in all the right ways.

God's Man

Though God's man in this passage is specifically the prophet Isaiah, what I'm about to write is more for my fellow church leaders, though it is just as applicable to any Christian in a position of influence or leadership. It's instructive that much of what God says to Isaiah is, in the Hebrew, second person plural.

God is telling Isaiah to lead the way, to exhibit what he says to the band gathered around him. And in doing so, he will enlist the fear-full fearlessness and dread-full dreadlessness of his prophetic band.

Let me emphasize it by calling attention to the plural pronouns and verbs: "You (plural) are not to call conspiracy all that this people call conspiracy, and their fears are not to be your (plural) fears, nor are you (plural) to dread. Rather, it is Yahweh of hosts you (plural) shall regard as holy and let him be your (plural) fear and your (plural) dread."

To put it sermonically, God's hand on God's man is for the good of God's people. As God's hand on God's man fortifies, corrects, and steadies him, thus sobering him, it communicates that good sense and right-mindedness to God's people. And they, then, can be freed from fearing and dreading what their community fears and dreads.

I bring this up because not only does Isaiah 8 imply the connection between God's man and God's people, but in the New Testament, Paul's emphasis on sober-mindedness is mostly in the pastoral letters. I have pondered this for several years and have become convinced Paul's thought is that as God's sobering hand is on God's man, it communicates sobriety—a life of good sense and right-mindedness—to God's people. The reverse of this comes easily to mind. When there are panicky pastors and elders, it is no wonder God's people become panicky.

When a congregation's leadership sees conspiracies and persecutions lurking behind every bush, it doesn't take long for God's people to become unsettled and agitated and understand themselves as victims. And once God's leaders and God's people are captured by panic, they say and do rotten things. They make bad choices. Once more, in the words of Os Guinness, "Those who *perceive* themselves as victims and respond by *portraying* themselves as victims end by *paralyzing* themselves as victims."[7]

But to press home the positive side of my point, as the Apostle Paul catalogs the qualities of a good church leader, he emphatically states that God's man[8] is to be sober-minded (1

Tim. 3:2[9]. See also Titus 1:8). Those who lead are to display a sense of sobriety and not to be prone to the panic and paranoia of a given era or aeon. As we saw in Titus, sober-mindedness is what liberating grace teaches us, and therefore, it is one trait that is in accord with healthy doctrine (Titus 2:1–14). If you want sober-minded people, then the leaders will sober-mindedly lead from the front in this regard.

Further, when Paul seeks to encourage and help Timothy, he writes to him in his final letter:

> For this reason I remind you to fan into flame the gift of God, which is in you through the laying on of my hands, for God gave us a spirit not of fear but of power and love and self-control (sophronismou). (2 Tim. 1:6–7)

As Timothy follows through and fans the flame of God's gift to him (likely his ordination as Paul's ministerial representative), he should do so with straight-on confidence because God did not give him, or Paul, a spirit of timidity and faintheartedness. Instead, God gave them the three-fold gift of power-love-sobriety. Paul may well have had Isaiah 8:11–13 in mind when he wrote that verse. God's man on whom is God's hand is not to walk about in the fear and dread of his neighborhood but to flourish in God's three-fold gift, which includes being in his right mind. So it is no surprise, then, that Paul comes back around to this thought toward the end of that same letter using a synonymous Greek word. He writes: *"As for you, always be sober-minded* (napho), *endure suffering, do the work of an evangelist, fulfill your ministry"* (2 Tim. 4:5).

God's sobering hand on God's sober man is for the good of God's sober-minded people. A right-minded leadership disperses an atmosphere of right-mindedness for the congregation to thrive in and flourish with.

This principle applies in a different direction as well. Paul guides the young man, Timothy, toward another aspect of being sober-minded when he writes in the same letter, *"So flee youthful passions and pursue righteousness, faith, love, and peace, along with those who call on the Lord from a pure heart"* (2 Tim. 2:22). If Timothy has been gifted with a sober mind, he is to have the good sense not to give into youthful passions. I'm sure Paul recognized youthful passions as including sexual urges. But those aren't the only youthful passions out there. It doesn't take much thought and reflection on one's own past youthful passions and indiscretions to see that this prohibition includes the youthful lust for thrill, sparkling adventures, impatience, longing for quick changes, immediate successes, restless adventures, and so forth. As Dennis Okholm observes:

> We modern-day gyrovagues believe the "grass is greener" in *another* marriage or church or vocation or geographical location. The trouble is that it often turns out to be the same hue. But it's not that the hue remains the same; *we* remain the same. Conversion and growth happen when we remain, not when we run (which is precisely what the ancients associated with *acedia*— a cowardly running away).[10]

Sober-minded church leaders grow and exude a sense of contentment that gives a congregation an opportunity to settle down and not get worn out racing after the newest ecclesiastical and social fads and schemes.

Instead of being constantly agitated, running day and night to this big adventure and that excitement, Timothy is to race after righteousness, faith, love, and peace. He is called to do so in company with others who desire the same qualities. Which means, then, that Timothy's right-minded approach will foster patience, as he learns to have *"nothing to do with foolish, ignorant controversies;… that… breed quarrels"* for:

> *The Lord's servant must not be quarrelsome but kind to everyone, able to teach, patiently enduring evil, correcting his opponents with gentleness.*

> *God may perhaps grant them repentance leading to a knowledge of the truth, and they may come to their senses and escape from the snare of the devil, after being captured by him to do his will.* (2:23–26)

This often mundane task of returning day after day to the routines of prayer, studies, visiting, forgiving, and teaching in the companionship of the same community nurtures a healthier mind and heart. It helps to cultivate a sober life, not only for the pastor but also the parishioners.

A sober-minded leadership aids a sober-minded church. When the congregational leadership is not swallowed up and swept away by the panic and alarm of the week but can thoughtfully see how we are to live out faithfulness to the Lord no matter what—then a church is truly enriched. Likewise, when pastors and elders refuse to be driven by youthful passions but flourish in a spirit of power, love, and sobriety—it builds up a congregation's durability in a stormy age.

God's sobering hand on God's sober man is for the good of God's sober-minded people.

As I finish up this chapter, allow me to go from preaching to meddling. Are you a pastor, preacher, priest, mother, father, teacher, professor, manager, or doctor? Are you someone in a role of influence and responsibility leading others? If so, then it will be good to pause and ask yourself the following questions:

What atmosphere are you giving your people to breathe?

Are you calling conspiracy what our age calls conspiracy, and dreading what they dread?

Are you fearing anything other than, or more than, the God and Father of our Lord Jesus Christ?

Are you living in fear and stimulating fear in your people?

Alternatively, are you chasing after youthful passions, longing and yearning for excitement and glamorous success, and therefore, constantly restless?

If you find yourself answering yes, then join me in turning

away from these to the One who has not given us a spirit of timidity, but has graciously given us the spirit of power, love and right-mindedness. Flourish in the grace and sovereignty of God, and so, always be sober-minded, endure suffering, do the work of an evangelist, and fulfill your ministry. God's sobering hand on God's sober man is good for God's sober-minded people.

Assess and Then Apply

These initial chapters have demonstrated the biblical concept of sober-mindedness and sobriety. The central portrait is grounded in our Lord and his calming the stormy sea and the stormy soul. There we found that Jesus' "Peace! Be still" conquered the squall of creation and brought rest to the restless, so that the previously restless one was found sitting, clothed and in his right mind. If we will keep this portrait at the forefront, we will have a good indication of real sobriety.

Next, we looked into two passages that chart the path of Christian conduct, where we live in accord with sound doctrine (Titus 2) and as new-made priests who have a new way of engaging relationally inside and outside of the church (Rom. 12:1–15:13). In both passages we discovered the crucial place of sober judgment and sobriety for every age group, social position, and sex. And in both, it was clear that the centrality of God's grace and Gospel are the very source of power for a sober life (Rom. 12:1–3; Titus 2:11–14).

Finally, we took time to learn from Isaiah as Yahweh's strong hand was on him, to secure, correct, and give him an assuring dread. Then, taking our lead from Isaiah 8:11–13, we noticed how important is a sober-minded leadership for a sober-minded congregation and came away with this principle: God's sobering hand on God's sober man is good for God's sober-minded people. At this point we turn a corner and delve into some suggestive examples of how to be a sober-minded people. The following subjects do not exhaust all angles of living soberly, but they do give us an idea. Addressed will be the topics of courage and *acedia*, dual citizenship, racism, the works of the flesh, and truth-telling. The final chapter will, hopefully, leave us lifted up as we are carried on eagle's wings.

---

1. Alice Marriot, *Ten Grandmothers: Epic of the Kiowas*, 196–205.
2. Sally Fitzgerald, *The Habit of Being*, 229.
3. Os Guinness, *Carpe Diem Redeemed*, 92.
4. Marilynne Robinson, "Fear."
5. Ibid.
6. Carmen Joy Imes, *Bearing God's Name*, 79.
7. Op. Cit.
8. All of the Greek adjectives in 1 Timothy 3:2–4 are in the masculine.
9. Paul places two sober-minded words together, *naphalion* and *sophrona*, laying a heady and heavy stress on living a life of sobriety at many levels. As we noted earlier, that's what happens in 1 Peter 4:8ff.
10. Dennis Okholm, *Dangerous Passions, Deadly Sins*, 149.

COURAGE

The LORD ruled as King as the floodwaters raged,
And still shall the LORD throughout every age.
The LORD will the strength of His people increase;
The LORD gives His people the blessing of peace.

—John Roberts, "You Sons of the Gods"

Henry Box Brown is a name you've likely never run across, but he was a real flesh-and-blood man who exhibited some knuckle-cracking courage. A slave in Richmond Virginia, he braved a harrowing condition to bring about his own liberation.

In 1849, at the age of thirty three, he lit on a way to escape slavery by having himself—with the help of anti-slavery friends—shipped in a crate less than two and a half feet deep, two feet wide, and three feet long. From the time he entered the box and was shipped to the moment of his emancipation in Philadelphia, he spent over twenty six hours in there. He was cramped, often turned wrong side up, moved around, packed away, and shuffled between various modes of transport. He and the crate were finally delivered to the office of the Philadelphia Vigilance Society.

As soon as Brown was released from his boxy confines, he stood up, greeted those around him and then remarked that "Before leaving Richmond he had selected for his arrival-hymn (if he lived)" the metered version of Psalm 40, "I waited patiently for the Lord, and he heard my prayer." Then, he began singing with relief and to the delight of his benefactors.[1]

Henry Box Brown was a man of daring and courage. Clearly, his courage was spawned by his faith in a God who could deliver. Brown's tale is a good place to begin thinking about how faith-filled courage fits with being sober-minded as we examine 1 Samuel 13–14. But before we go too far, it will be useful to touch on a preliminary observation.

One pitfall in reading the Old Testament is to read it like we would read Aesop's Fables, always looking for a moral to the story. If this is how we approach the Hebrew scriptures, then it creates some uncomfortable problems.

An important key to grasping the Old Testament is to see that what is descriptive is not necessarily prescriptive. Sometimes we are only being told what happened. We're not to go and do like-wise. At other times, we are wading through an episode, and God intends it to change our conduct. How can you tell if a story is simply descriptive or if it is being prescriptive?

First, you look at a scene or episode through God's clear directions in other places. Second, you look for the divine diagnosis in the story.

As an example, Solomon had seven hundred wives and three hundred concubines, most of whom were not followers of Yahweh. We know from Genesis 2:21–24 (and our Lord's statement in Matthew 19:3–6) that polygamy is not prescribed by God. Therefore, we are not to go and do likewise. But also, not only does Scripture in many places forbid marrying outside of the boundary lines of his people (principle: Christians are to only marry Christians), but in the story of Solomon's married life in 1 Kings 11, the warning comes through loud and clear:

> *He had 700 wives, who were princesses, and 300 concubines. And his wives turned away his heart. For when Solomon was old his wives turned away his heart after other gods, and his heart was not wholly true to the LORD his God, as was the heart of David his father.* (1 Kings 11:3–4)

The prescription, hammered home in this most disheartening episode, is sharp—don't marry outside the faith.

Nevertheless, the Old Testament stories are meant to be guides, and they are given to us as examples. Paul repeatedly says this in places like 1 Corinthians 10:1–11 and Romans 15:4. Their exhibition of resilient faith, even in precarious situations, is displayed in all of its grandeur in Hebrews 11. With this in mind, we turn to an event that happened in 1 Samuel 13–14, where we meet two men, a father and his son.

This father and son share some family traits: 1) impatience with dwindling, disheartening circumstance; and b) a willingness to take initiative. But in the end, there are different outcomes. One of these men receives God's displeasure. The other becomes the means of the LORD's salvation and rescue. What's the difference between them?

Situation

In 1 Samuel 13:1–8, we meet the situation that confronted both men. The kingdom of God is being resisted, and the opposition has drawn together their enormous numbers and horrendous hordes to stand against God's reign. There are thousands upon thousands of fearsome, frightful, fierce men of war brandishing their newest, cutting-edge technological weaponry. We read:

> And the Philistines mustered to fight with Israel, thirty thousand chariots
> and six thousand horsemen and troops like the sand on the seashore in
> multitude.... So on the day of the battle there was neither sword nor
> spear found in the hand of any of the people with Saul and Jonathan
> (13:5, 22)

It's a knee-knocking, gut-rending, impressive scene. Sure enough, the people of God are filled with trepidation, consternation, and apprehension. In that day when combat would have been primarily the up-close-and-personal type of hand-to-hand combat, they were overwhelmed not only in numbers but in their perception and in their faith. It was an impossible state of affairs. And so, in the swamping tide of impending catastrophe, there's a mass church-exodus (13:8). The numbers have shrunk down to the point of unbearable. There is no way six hundred (13:15) low-tech, out-gunned, out-supplied warriors can stand against the multiple thousands of highly equipped, heavily armed, and heftily fortified soldiers of the Philistines (13:19–23). The handwriting is on the wall. And it's here that the father and son respond in similar and dissimilar ways.

Saul

Apparently, Samuel, God's spokesperson, had instructed Saul to set up camp at a specific place. God gave him a seven-day window (13:8a). Possibly, the prophet Samuel was orchestrating the call up of reservists and the National Guard during that time. But as each day and hour grinds by, Saul is getting more and more desperate. Then the day comes when Samuel should have appeared, but there's no Samuel! The people are scattering and scampering off, and there's no Samuel to show that this is God's battle that will end in God's victory. What is a body to do in such distressing times?

In desperation, Saul exposes the family traits (13:9–15a). He takes matters into his own hands. Something must be done. The pressure is intense, and the desertions are irreparable.

Maybe the troops were murmuring and muttering under their breath or to one another that Saul was running people off or that he had lost his nerve. Whatever the case, it was a most disturbing moment (13:11–12). So, Saul rises up, steps out, and takes action.

But the action he takes is all wrong.

Instead of waiting for the arrival of God's spokesperson, and thus waiting for God's shepherding, sustaining, and saving Word, Saul soothed his conscience with religious rebellion. As becomes increasingly clear in the rest of his life, Saul's religion is only about fabricating fortune, inciting encouragement, and directing destiny. Saul's deed here shows that he thought pragmatically—if it works, just do it. His actions point out his belief that some emergencies simply made God's Word unnecessary.

At just that moment, lo and behold, Samuel arrives. You can imagine the little voices in Saul's head might have gasped and said, "Busted!" Samuel announces God's diagnosis of Saul's action:

> *You have done foolishly. You have not kept the command of the LORD your God, with which he commanded you. For then the LORD would have established your kingdom over Israel forever. But now your kingdom shall not continue. The LORD has sought out a man after his own heart, and the LORD has commanded him to be prince over his people, because you have not kept what the LORD commanded you.* (13:13–14)

A similar divine diagnosis is aired just two chapters later when Saul's half-hearted, half-way obedience (which is thus, disobedience) is outed by God, and he declares:

> *Has the LORD as great delight in burnt offerings and sacrifices, as in obeying the voice of the LORD? Behold, to obey is better than sacrifice, and*

> *to listen than the fat of rams. For rebellion is as the sin of divination, and*
> *presumption is as iniquity and idolatry. Because you have rejected the word*
> *of the LORD, he has also rejected you from being king.* (1 Sam.
> 15:22–23)

Saul is a man of impatience and initiative, and he is only using his religion for his own ends. God's discovering diagnosis of Saul is precise. Even Saul acknowledges the accuracy of God's analysis in his confessions of his sin in chapter 13 and 15. But unfortunately in both cases, he makes excuses for his actions:

> *When I saw that the people were scattering from me, and that you did not*
> *come within the days appointed,… the people spared the best of the sheep*
> *and of the oxen to sacrifice to the LORD your God, and the rest we have*
> *devoted to destruction.* (13:1,1 15:15)

Observe the glaring gap between Saul's confession and David's later confession in Psalm 51. David makes no excuses but draws the genuine guilt rightly onto himself.[2] What we see in Saul, among other things, can be classed as *acedia*.

Some years back while I was preparing for a Sunday morning sermon, I tripped over a piece written by Dorothy Sayers, a Christian writer who was a contemporary with C. S. Lewis. Her words forced me to pause and read them over several times. She writes:

> The sixth Deadly Sin is named by the Church *Acedia* or *Sloth*. In
> the world it calls itself Tolerance; but in hell it is called Despair. It
> is the accomplice of the other sins and their worst punishment. It
> is the sin which believes in nothing, cares for nothing, seeks to
> know nothing, interferes with nothing, enjoys nothing, loves
> nothing, hates nothing, finds purpose in nothing, lives for
> nothing, and only remains alive because there is nothing it would
> die for.[3]

The sluggish hopelessness of *acedia* is not necessarily physical laziness, though it can show up there. It's that state of mind and heart that can suck the life out of courage and flow into a despair of purpose, conscious rejection of joy or a flourishing cynicism about people or God. It can be as persistent as a dogged West Texas weed that refuses to be snuffed out no matter how much drought it goes through or Round-Up is applied. And it shrugs its shoulders and sighs with an apathetic "Whatever."

Yet, more deadly than all the above, is what Peter Leithart notes when he writes, "Sloth is a lack of faith in God's providence and care and a lack of hope that God will keep his promises."[4] Unable or unwilling to trust that what God has spoken with his mouth he will fulfill with his hand (1 Kings 8:15, 24), we can end up hunkering down into disillusionment, apathy, shiftlessness, lethargic, empty heartedness, and empty soulishness.[5] This sloth manifests itself in two different forms. It can be a form of laziness, but it can also show up as feverish activity, and restless wondering that neglect spiritual readings and prayer, "substituting a task-oriented life."[6]

And so, whether it exhibits itself in listlessness or restlessness, in either case, it shows up in a soul that has lost the satisfaction of joy within and pursues sources of consolation from without. It is opposed to "the joy of love. It is, simply, running from God and all goodness."[7] Acedia is the turning of our hearts away from God to our conditions, and caving into them. This caving into our conditions can turn into listlessness or it can follow Saul into a faithless pragmatism.

Pastors struggle with *acedia*. There they are, preaching the Gospel of Jesus, administering the sacraments, and praying days and years on end. But when they see little fruit that fulfills their expectations,[8] they give up the important apostolic calling of continuing in prayer and the ministry of the Word (Acts 6:4). They are tempted to scrap the laborious task of studying and preparing to preach the tough stuff of God's whole counsel. They might try to fill up the void with pollyanna-ish, positive-mental-attitude success messages that help almost no one deal with deadly tornadoes, floods, drought, death, persecution, injustice, tsunamis, abuse, self-damage, sin, or with God himself.

They may move over to another dangerous extreme. They might seek to force God to keep their esoteric timelines. Maybe they will endeavor to compel God to do "mighty works in our time" by stringing together biblical incantations that bully God into their own will, a will to prosper and a will to power. Then again, they may strive to push God to take notice of their "ministry" by means of ecstatic enthusiasms that look strangely like the Ba'al priests on Mount Carmel (1 Kings 18).

In whatever way it fleshes out, the root disease is the same —*acedia*, sloth. Unable to believe any longer that God keeps faith with his people, they are deflated and disillusioned by numerous defeats and disappointments. All that is left is "whatever." Nature abhorring a vacuum as it does, the void that once was faith becomes the sink hole that swallows down any and every technique that will make one feel good or successful. A deadly sin indeed. But wait, there's another man somewhere around Michmash. It's Saul's son Jonathan.

Son

The scene is the same. The circumstances are still just as discouraging and distressing. The future looks bleak for God's people, and the opposition is overwhelming. Jonathan exhibits the family traits when he rallies his armor bearer:

> Come, let us go over to the garrison of these uncircumcised. It may be that the LORD will work for us, for nothing can hinder the LORD from saving by many or by few. (14.1, 6)

Jonathan also rises up, steps out, and takes action, but there is a clear difference. Saul tried to use God to create his fortune and success. Jonathan relied on God. Jonathan's conviction that God can save with many or few produced a daring expectation and expedition (14:6). Saul's religious rebellion showed his unbelief. Jonathan's daring brilliantly declared his trust in the God of Abraham, Isaac, and Jacob. It was a trust in the truth about God, that he is not regulated and reduced by creaturely limitations or circumstantial shortages. Jonathan had a heart that was much like good king Jehosophat's a few hundred years later: *"His heart was courageous in the ways of the LORD"* (2 Chron. 17:6a).

Further, Jonathan's trust is satisfied with whatever God decides to do. Jonathan is content with God and has no need to control him. God can save by many or by a few. But then again, he just might choose not to rescue ("It may be..." v. 6). God is not bound and chained by Jonathan's faith or ferocity. Therefore, Jonathan can rest on the promises of God since he knows that God is bigger, grander, and unchained.

He is not a god of magic. He is not a god of the *quid pro quo* (my little bit of this for God's great big that). And Yahweh is not the errand-boy god!

What is the divine verdict on Jonathan's decision? We read, *"So the LORD saved Israel that day"* (14:23). In the words of Dr. Dale Ralph Davis,

> Jonathan was right: "Nothing can keep Yahweh from saving by many or by few." (v. 6b). This salvation, however, did not begin in royal mathematics (13:15b; 14:2) but with imaginative faith, faith that was willing to say, "Perhaps Yahweh will act for us."[9]

In his impatience and initiative, a father tried to use God to his ends and successes. In his impatience and initiative, a son trusted in God, come what may. One was ruled by his fears, worries, and "likes" on his profile page. The other was found, so to speak, sitting, clothed, and in his right mind. One could only be afraid, while the other was heartened by the storm-calming Savior and squall-conquering Sovereign.

These two stories, or two parts of the same story, are important personally as well as regarding a sober-minded life. I am a "take-action" guy, especially in the face of dwindling, discouraging, desperate situations. I want to be the Nike poster boy, the Just Do It guy reaping heaps of success and accomplishments.

Reading these two chapters causes me to pull up short and hesitate. Not any old Just-Do-It-ism will suffice. I need God's Word, and there is no emergency or pride that can trump it. But I also need a daring heart, a heart like good king Jehosophat's: *"His heart was courageous in the ways of the LORD"* (2 Chron. 17:6a). Like Jonathan and Henry Box Brown, I need a faith-filled heart that is courageous in believing that God can save, rescue, and deliver with a large or an itty-bitty number. But I must also be courageous enough to trust him even if he chooses not to work for us in this moment, or this season. Here is an important aspect of a life of sobriety.

Kevin J. Vanhoozer touches on this sober-minded Jonathan-like trust as he addresses what he calls "eschatological discipleship." He notes, "Disciples who have learned where they are in the biblical story will have a sense of urgency, not anxiety, about the future."[10]

Like Jonathan, a sober mind may have an urgency about it, but it can put the anxiety aside. It can set over in the corner that heartless, hopeless agitation and the angst of *acedia*. It can step out in defiant faith that God is faithful to himself, to his promises, and to his people. And that he will sweep up our successes, failures and partial feats and pour them into his kingdom come! In the seminal words of Andrew Solomon, as he unpacked *acedia*:

> When you are depressed, you need the love of other people, and yet depression fosters actions that destroy that love. Depressed

people often stick pins into their own life rafts. The conscious mind can intervene. One is not helpless.[11]

We can do this because the grace of God is *"training us to renounce ungodliness and worldly passions, and to live self-controlled* (sophronos), *upright, and godly lives in the present age"* (Titus 2:12).

After reading 1 Samuel 13–14, it would be good to take a moment and reflect:

- Are there ways you find Saul's and Jonathan's family traits echoing in your soul? If so, does impatience and initiative lead you to try to use God, or to trust him?
- How do you respond to dwindling, disheartening situations? Do you find that the weed of *acedia* has wrapped itself around the tree of your faith to choke it out?
- Does God's sovereignty, majesty, and fidelity give you courage even in the face of discouragement?
- Have you met, and come to know, the storm-calming Savior and squall-conquering Sovereign? The One *"who for the joy that was set before him endured the cross, despising the shame, and is seated at the right hand of the throne of God"* (Heb. 12:2).
- If so, are you considering *"him who endured from sinners such hostility against himself, so that you may not grow weary or fainthearted"* (13:3)?
- Finally, are you prepared to care about things and especially the things of God? If so, ask God to give you a heart like King Jehoshaphat's and Jonathan's; a heart *"courageous in the ways of the LORD"* (2 Chron. 17:6a).

---

1. Christine Rudisel and Bob Blaisdell, *Slave Narratives*, 1–5.

2. This comparison between Saul and David was brought to my attention by Gene Overton, a friend and elder at First Reformed Presbyterian Church in Minco, Oklahoma.

3. Dorothy L. Sayers, *Christian Letters*, 152.

4. Peter J. Leithart, *1 & 2 Kings*, 114.

5. Sayers, Op. Cit., 153.

6. Okholm, Op. Cit., 143–4.

7. Ibid., 152.

8. Expectations, which are often foisted on them by Seminaries, Church Planting conferences, Denominational moguls, and Church-Growth gurus, to name a few.

9. Dale Ralph Davis, *1 Samuel: Looking on the Heart*, 139.

10. Kevin J. Vanhoozer, *Hearers & Doers*, 68.

11. Andrew Solomon, *The Noonday Demon*, 110.

STRANGERS IN A STRANGE LAND

Fear him, ye saints, and you will then
have nothing else to fear;
make you his service your delight;
he'll make your wants his care.

—Tate and Brady,
"Through All the Changing Scenes of Life"

We were young and had only been married eighteen months when I got stationed at Incirlik Air Base in Turkey. It was a new experience in a country where customs, language, expectations, smells, and timekeeping were all different from what I grew up with. During those two years, my wife and I were constantly reminded that we were the foreigners and strangers. Not that the nationals rubbed it in. Most of them were gracious and glad to help us.

While we were stationed there we also went on a trip to Greece and another to Germany. The experiences were the same.

We were the strangers and outlanders meandering through unfamiliar places, peoples, practices, and patois. Foreigners in foreign places.

Christians need to remember something that is often difficult to keep in mind. We are dual citizens, and this creates for us a weirdness and tension that we want changed and fixed. But resolving it by going too far in either direction places us in a perilous situation.

Our true reality is voiced in the words of Moses: *"I have been a stranger in a strange land"* (Exod 2:22 KJV). The idea of being resident aliens, outlanders, foreigners, or strangers is a motif that runs through Scripture for God's church in both the Old and New Testament.

This was God's characterization of Israel in the wilderness: *"The land shall not be sold in perpetuity, for the land is mine. For you are strangers and sojourners with me"* (Lev. 25:23).

It's Peter's description of God's people, *"Beloved, I urge you as sojourners and exiles to abstain from the passions of the flesh, which wage war against your soul"* (1 Peter 1:1, 17; 2:11).

And yet, we strangers and exiles are also *"no longer strangers and aliens, but you are fellow citizens with the saints and members of the household of God"* (Eph. 2:19).

So, having this dual citizenship and recognizing that we are strangers in a strange land is who we are. How does this impact what we do? After just a quick glance at the passages mentioned above in their context, it becomes clear we are to be compassionate toward other displaced people since we are God's displaced people (Lev. 25:23–24; as well as 19:33-34), and we're to live differently (1 Peter 2:11–12). Retaining this dual citizenship in our thoughts, actions, and decisions is another aspect of having our heads on straight. Jeremiah 29 presents us with a real example of what it looks like to be strangers in a strange land.

Strangers

Jeremiah 29 begins by explaining that it is a letter written to a specific body of people:

> *These are the words of the letter that Jeremiah the prophet sent from Jerusalem to the surviving elders of the exiles, and to the priests, the prophets, and all the people, whom Nebuchadnezzar had taken into exile from Jerusalem to Babylon.* (29:1)

A certain group of God's people have been uprooted and hauled off to a new land, a place that is not the homeland promised to them. Unmistakably, this is a result of the multi-generational failure of God's people and their breaking faith with God. And though this specific group to whom Jeremiah writes has been part of the faith-breaking community, there is something different about them. To see exactly what's going on, we will need to take a short jump back to chapter 24.

In Jeremiah 24, the prophet sees a vision of two baskets with two different kinds of figs. There are the good figs, the people sent into exile when Jeconiah, King of Judah was taken away (24:4–7). And there are the bad figs, those hanging on to king Zedekiah and their homeland to the end (24:8–10). The good figs are the very same group to whom the letter in chapter 29 is written (29:2).

What is truly astounding is that Yahweh says he has made this specific band of "figs" strangers, exiles, for their own good. They will actually benefit deeply from the experience:

> *Like these good figs, so I will regard as good the exiles from Judah, whom I have sent away from this place to the land of the Chaldeans. I will set my eyes on them for good, and I will bring them back to this land. I will build them up, and not tear them down; I will plant them, and not pluck them up. I will give them a heart to know that I am the LORD, and they shall be my*

people and I will be their God, for they shall return to me with their whole heart. (24:5–7)

The bad figs will end up experiencing exile later, and it will be a decimating encounter (24:8–10).

Since both groups were part of Judah and both were involved in the breach of Yahweh's covenant, then the quality of the figs has less to do with them and more to do with God's analysis and arrangement. We have pictured for us what Paul will describe later: *"What shall we say then? Is there injustice on God's part? By no means!"* For he says to Moses:

I will have mercy on whom I have mercy, and I will have compassion on whom I have compassion." So then it depends not on human will or exertion, but on God, who has mercy. For the Scripture says to Pharaoh, "For this very purpose I have raised you up, that I might show my power in you, and that my name might be proclaimed in all the earth." So then he has mercy on whomever he wills, and he hardens whomever he wills. (Rom. 9:14–18)

The letter of Jeremiah 29 is written to the good figs whom Yahweh sent into exile for their own good. God has made them strangers in a strange land because he has set his eyes on them for good. He will build them up and not tear them down, plant them and not pluck them up. In fact, he will give them a new heart to know Yahweh and to return to him with their whole heart. God's aim for them helps us to read better his plans for them in chapter 29.

Strange Land

Through the prophet, Yahweh gives guidelines to the good figs on how they should respond to their expatriation. Recall that this time of expulsion from the land of the promise is for their good, and God has designs on what he intends for them (24:5–7). Toward that objective, as they wait for Yahweh to come and take them home, they are to press onward into four areas as strangers in this strange land.

First, they are to build and develop, to be fruitful and multiply (29:5–6). Instead of hunkering down, licking their wounds, bemoaning the horrible fate that has befallen them, decrying their minority status, and lamenting the moral decadence of the society around them, they are to be constructive people. They are to be engaged in normal, day-in-day-out activities of production and procreation. All of this is an act of faith, a flesh-and-blood trust that what the reliable God says the reliable God does. Yahweh will be true to them and come and take them home one day as he promised (29:10). Even though the land is not their homeland, the country is not their country, and the leadership is not their chosen package of candidates, they are to straighten up and raise their heads, knowing that their redemption is drawing near (Luke 21:28).

Further, their activities will benefit the pagans, and so bring themselves benefit. We read:

> But seek the welfare of the city where I have sent you into exile, and pray to the LORD on its behalf, for in its welfare you will find your welfare. (29:7)

As they seek the *shalom* (peace, welfare, well-being) of the city, they too will be filled up with Yahweh's *shalom*. Their own welfare as strangers is tied up with the city's in this strange land. Oddly enough, this will be reciprocal *shalom*. As they benefit this strange land, they will be benefited, which will benefit the city, and so forth. God's strangers are beneficial for the strange land to which they have been exiled.

Then Yahweh warns them not to get sidetracked by the naysayers, doomsdayers, prognosticators, and soothsayers who spread fear and gloom (29:8–9). Later in this letter, Yahweh will specifically mention and denounce three certain side-trackers by name (29:21–31). These talking heads have sent their own missives. They are trying to shut down the prophet and seeking to rouse some kind of resistance movement. Yahweh denounces their lies and rebellion, and he uncovers their indecencies because Yahweh is "the one who knows" and is witness against them (29:23). Therefore, he tells them not to let these broadcasters get them side-tracked and off course.

Finally, Yahweh gives them the heart of his whole program—have hope in God's rescue (29:10). Though that rescue will include Yahweh's return to take them home, it contains even more. We read:

> For I know the plans I have for you, declares the LORD, plans for welfare (shalom) and not for evil, to give you a future and a hope. Then you will call upon me and come and pray to me, and I will hear you. You will seek me and find me, when you seek me with all your heart. I will be found by you, declares the LORD, and I will restore your fortunes and gather you.... (29:11–14)

Look for God's rescue. Live on, day after day, into the hope of God's rescue since he has made us strangers in a strange land to do us good, change us, and revive us.

One more note before moving forward. Daniel was one of those who was taken off into captivity sometime before the letter was written (Dan. 1:1, 3–4). Though Jeremiah's letter of chapter 29 is never referred to,[1] Daniel and his three friends were there when it was sent, and they are illustrative of God's strangers seeking the welfare, the *shalom*, of the city. One wonders if Jeremiah's letter encouraged them and gave them their marching orders.

Sober-Minded

So, what does this all have to do with being sober-minded, living a life of sobriety, and having our heads on straight? I'm hopeful that much of what this passage says to us will be obvious. But here I draw out a few thoughts to aid us.

As Christians, we must always remember that we are strangers in a strange land. For all the ways the old hymn seems to get it wrong, in a very profound way this song got it all right. For:

> *This world is not my home*
> *I'm just a passing through*
> *My treasures are laid up somewhere beyond the blue*
> *The angels beckon me from heaven's open door*
> *And I can't feel at home in this world anymore*
> *Oh Lord you know I have no friend like you*
> *If heaven's not my home then Lord what will I do*
> *The angels beckon me from heaven's open door*
> *And I can't feel at home in this world anymore.*[2]

The Apostle Peter maps this sentiment out in 1 Peter 2:9–17. Because of God's grace in Jesus Christ, we have been made God's chosen race, royal priesthood, holy nation, his special treasure. Therefore, we are—by God's making—sojourners and exiles who must:

> *Abstain from the passions of the flesh, which wage war against your soul. Keep your conduct among the Gentiles honorable, so that when they speak against you as evildoers, they may see your good deeds and glorify God on the day of visitation.* (2:11–12)

This means that we have been made strangers in a strange land for our good, and thus, we should seek the *shalom* of "the city," which is what Peter describes in 2:13–17. This "stranger in a strange land" vocation that seeks the *shalom* of "the city" is "the will of God" for us, so:

> *That by doing good you should put to silence the ignorance of foolish people. Live as people who are free, not using your freedom as a cover-up for evil, but living as servants of God.* (2:15–16)

Or, as the writer of Hebrews would have us understand, we are like Abraham *"looking forward to the city that has foundations, whose designer and builder is God"* (Hebr. 11:10). And, like Abel, Noah, Abraham, and Sarah, we may die, but we should die in faith that what the reliable God says the reliable God does. Therefore, though not yet receiving the fulfillment of all that God promises in Jesus, we see those promises and greet them from afar, acknowledging that we are, for the moment:

> *Strangers and exiles on the earth. For people who speak thus make it clear that they are seeking a homeland. If they had been thinking of that land from which they had gone out, they would have had opportunity to return. But as it is, they desire a better country, that is, a heavenly one. Therefore God is not ashamed to be called their God, for he has prepared for them a city.* (Hebr. 11:13–16)

And yet at the same time, we are to love our country. We seek the *shalom* of the country, prospering it, praying for it, living responsibly in it, serving it—including entering the military, civil service, and so on. We end up prospering neighbors whether they are Christians or not, and so we are prospered ourselves.

We live, work, raise children, educate them, clean our houses, and mow our yards. We pray for our leaders, whether we voted for them or not. In this regard, since our Lord has told us to love our enemies, and pray for even the ones who persecute us, *"so that you may be sons of your Father who is in heaven"* (Matt. 5:44–45), it is worth asking if you prayed for our previous president and his family and are you praying for the present president and his family? Are you praying for them in ways similar to how you pray for your mother and father, grandparents and children?[3]

We can do all of this with the sure and certain knowledge that we have a future, one when Christ returns and the meek inherit the earth. We are to love our country, and as we prosper our land, we will be prospered. All of this is possible because the grace of God is *"training us to renounce ungodliness and worldly passions, and to live self-controlled* (sophronos)*, upright, and godly lives in the present age"* (Titus 2:12).

Toward the end of the second century, a chap named Diognetus received a letter from a Christian. It was a letter defending Christians and Christianity. In this letter the writer describes how ordinary Christians are even though they are also unordinary. He wrote:

> They inhabit both Greek and barbarian cities, according to the lot assigned to each. And they show forth the character of their own citizenship in a marvelous and admittedly paradoxical way by following local customs in what they wear and what they eat and in the rest of their lives. They live in their respective countries, but only as resident aliens; they participate in all things as citizens, and they endure all things as foreigners. Every foreign territory is a homeland for them, every homeland foreign territory.[4]

Dual citizenship. Strangers in a strange land.

To recognize that we are strangers in a strange land is important in staying in our right minds. As Richard John Neuhaus observed in his final book before he died:

> One derives from [Augustine's] writings, what is best described as an "Augustinian sensibility." It is the sensibility of the pilgrim

through time who resolutely resists the temptation to despair in the face of history's disappointments and tragedies, and just as resolutely declines the delusion of having arrived at history's end.[5]

To have this "Augustinian sensibility" roots us as the social storms rage and rip up the moral and social frameworks around us.

Johnny Cash sang an old song years ago about some religious folks who were so heavenly minded they were no earthly good. I get his point. But let me turn it inside-out. Scripture is calling us to become so heavenly minded that we can finally be some earthly good! That is one aspect of how to be in our right minds. To live, love, work, and play knowing that there's more than what the corporate world, advertisers, educators and politicians tell us there is.

Yes, we're strangers in a strange land for our good, and the wellbeing of the place we are in, but there's more coming, far more. Therefore, let us become so heavenly minded, we can finally become some earthly good!

Here at the end of the chapter is a fitting time to stop and pray. Maybe you could join me in this petition I have pulled together from several biblical passages and other sources. If you will, then let us pray:

Holy, holy, holy, is the Lord God Almighty, who was and is and is to come! Great and amazing are your deeds, O Lord God the Almighty! Just and true are your ways, O King of the nations! Who will not fear you, O Lord, and glorify your name? For you alone are holy. All nations will come and worship you, for your righteous acts have been revealed. We bow before you knowing that you have cared for us and will continue to do so. Your might and majesty are far above and beyond our comprehension or conceptions. We acknowledge and admire your works of providence, whereby your most holy, wise and powerful preserving and governing of all your creatures and all our actions is to your glory and to our good.

Confident in you, who has promised "I will never leave you nor forsake you," we boldly say, "The Lord is my helper; I will not fear; what can man do to me?" Therefore, knowing that you have plans for us, plans for our shalom and not for evil, to give us a future and a hope, help us to rise up trusting you, and to build houses and live in them; plant gardens and eat their produce. Take wives and have sons and daughters; take wives for our sons, and give our daughters in marriage, that they may bear sons and daughters; to multiply and not decrease. We seek the shalom of the city where you have sent us as strangers in a strange land, and we pray to you on its behalf, for in its shalom we will find our shalom.

O God, may justice roll down like waters, and righteousness like an ever-flowing stream. And may we, your people, be those who always humble ourselves under your mighty hand knowing that in due time you will raise us up; who cast all of our care on you who cares for us. Help us to have our heads on straight. Help us to become so heavenly minded we can be some real earthly good. Now to the King of the ages, immortal, invisible, the only God, be honor and glory forever and ever. Amen.

---

1. Though Jeremiah's prophecy of Babylon being in power 70 years, and at the end of the time, the LORD will return to his people, is referenced by Daniel (Jeremiah 25:11–12; 29:10; and Daniel 9:2).
2. Albert E. Brumley, "This World Is not My Home."
3. Examples of this can be found in two books by Charles Garriott—*Obama Prayers* and *Prayers for Trump*.
4. Loeb Classical Library, *Apostolic Fathers 2*, 139–40.
5. Richard John Neuhaus, *American Babylon*, 23.

IMAGERY AND NARRATIVE

Sign, sign, everywhere a sign
Blockin out the scenery, breakin my mind
Do this, don't do that, can't you read the sign?

—The 5 Man Electric Band, "Signs"

I had recently retired from twenty years in the Air Force and became the regular student preacher of this small-town church. He was one of my elders, in his late 70s. To my surprise he was appalled that I, his minister, had purchased a Toyota. When I asked him what was so wrong with having a Toyota, he replied, "It was made by the Japs!" Needless to say, I was startled by his comment, so I stammered my way through the question, "Why does that matter?"

The response was just as shocking as his statement. As he put it, he had grown up during World War II, and recounted how the government propaganda during the time hammered into him that the "Japs" were evil. And now there he was in 1999, some fifty four years later, and he still couldn't bring himself to purchase anything Japanese. Similar stories can be recounted from World War I and the way the imagery and narrative regarding the horrible "Huns" affected and infected social perceptions about Germans.

Imagery and narrative were coupled together and employed to speedily answer the "why" questions for both wars and to construct a ready resilience in the American population for the war-making machinery. This is an important concept to keep in mind when trying to decipher peoples' responses to various ideas.

It's important to ask: How have diverse media, agencies, governments, and movements merged imagery and narrative to pragmatically build consensus and results? A case in point is the use of the expression "racism" and its sibling expressions.

The term "racism" has been fused with portrayals and plot lines of lynchings, burning crosses, and bloodshed on the silver screen, television, print, newscasts, textbooks, and other platforms. There appear to me to be at least two results from this merger of imagery and narrative: 1) it "others" racism, "Why, that's what those other people do." And, in a different direction, 2) when saying that racism is still alive in our country and churches, the marriage of those images and accounts of lynchings and burning crosses burble up and evoke strong reactions that spawn a deafening defensiveness.

Add to these two results the way certain groups use the expression to shut down conversations or intimidate people who disagree with them and their particular religious/social agendas, then you can begin to understand why resistance becomes rampant. Ta-Nehisi Coates observed the connection between imagery and narrative back in 2008 when he wrote:

> In some measure, the narrowing of racism is an unfortunate relic
> of the civil rights movement, when activists got mileage out of

dehumanizing racists and portraying them as ultra-violent Southern troglodytes. Whites may have been horrified by the fire hoses and police dogs turned on children, but they could rest easy knowing that neither they nor anyone they'd ever met would do such a thing.[1]

It's a bit risky to address this subject knowing that I could be misunderstood. But I take the risk to present a specimen of one way being sober-minded can help to bring a wholesome orderliness to an environment that has been unsettled by external pressures. In the past few years there have been plenty of barbs of "racism" hurled about in churches and denominations. There have been strong pontifications flung over social media.

From where I sit, it feels at times as if the seams are beginning to unravel under the stress. Therefore, if we desire to reclaim and be reclaimed by sobriety, we should examine this subject from another angle. I would like to posit a different word and distinctive approach in hopes that it will foster a more sound-minded way of acknowledging and dealing with this important subject.

The Flesh

My suggestion is to place racism back inside the biblical continuum of "flesh." This is not to strip down or deny the reality the term is addressing or take away any of its importance. Rather, it is intended to give that concept a location inside a different narrative as part of an extensive storyline that has a Christ-centered remedy. Doing this will help show that what is often called racism and its resolution has been on God's radar for a far longer time than we or our fore-bearers have been around.

To make my case, I am going to approach this subject from two slightly different angles. To begin, I will take us to a different subject to gain an example.

Teamed Together

Christians normally affirm that, according to Scripture, sexual aberrations are sinful. And yet, to pull one erotic anomaly out of the biblical continuum and to obsess over it, preach against it every other Sunday, write simmering articles about it, and regularly demonstrate against it at state capitols creates an unhealthy over-emphasis. That unhealthy over-emphasis ends up forming an atmosphere that feels hostile to those trying to tackle and tame their sensual attractions. It also fosters the impression that the rest of us are okay (or that we think we're okay) because we don't engage in "that sin." Therefore, keeping peccadillos in their biblical context helps us to realize that when we point one finger at someone else, there are three more pointing back at us.

For instance, when Paul lists sins, he often teams them together. In 1 Corinthians 5 the Apostle has been dealing with a specific sexual deviation that was allowed to go on by some in that congregation (5:1–8). They were even quite proud of their tolerance and broad-minded approach. Paul tackles this issue, but then, in a surprising move, he turns the Corinthian church away from targeting one singular sexually immoral deed by itself, and he itemizes it along with greed, idolatry, reviling, drunkenness, and swindling (5:9–13). He does this again in the very next chapter:

> Or do you not know that the unrighteous will not inherit the kingdom of God? Do not be deceived: neither the sexually immoral, nor idolaters, nor adulterers, nor men who practice homosexuality, nor thieves, nor the greedy, nor drunkards, nor revilers, nor swindlers will inherit the kingdom of God. (1 Cor. 6:9–10)

Paul is pushing them (and us) to see that when one finger is pointed at someone else's sin there are likely three more pointing right back at us.

Or to put it in another way, when dealing with dirty laundry, the Apostle doesn't focus on one item of soiled clothing. The whole laundry basket is full, and all of it needs to be washed. It would be odd to obsess about a singular dirty garment, pull it out of the basket, rant against its filthiness, and ignore the other items in the hamper, some of which might just be mine. Paul teams together immoralities in several places. Look at Romans 1:18–32,[2] Ephesians 5:3–5, and Colossians 3:5–7.

Following the scriptural pattern of keeping vices generally teamed together helps save us from self-righteously thinking we're okay because we don't practice "that sin." Which then aids our churches to be redemptive, restorative fellowships for people who are overwhelmed by their own weakness. We're all in this sinking, stinking boat together, and we all need Jesus to save us! With this example in mind, we can now step over to my main thought.

Litany

The Scriptural category "flesh" encompasses a whole range of immoralities, iniquities, and injustices to include what we have come to call "racism." Here's how the apostle addresses it:

> Now the works of the flesh are evident: sexual immorality, impurity, sensuality, idolatry, sorcery, enmity, strife, jealousy, fits of anger, rivalries, dissensions, divisions, envy, drunkenness, orgies, and things like these. I warn you, as I warned you before, that those who do such things will not inherit the kingdom of God. (Gal. 5:19–21)

If we keep the storyline and emphasis of Galatians in mind, we can see how many of the different aspects of "racism" are mentioned in this litany called "the works of the flesh."

The issue that provoked Paul's ire and roused him to write this letter was that certain people who claimed Jesus as Lord also demanded of everyone else either ethnic assimilation or racial apartness. These Jewish disciples of the Messiah mandated that Gentile followers of Jesus had to believe in Jesus plus become Jewish. If they would not then they were to be placed outside of "our" fellowship.

One of the results is that this assimilation-or-apartness approach shattered communion. No longer were the Jewish disciples eating (communion?) with the Gentile disciples. They were pulled apart and the fault line was groupish, ethnic, and clannish (Gal. 2:11–14). As someone has recently mentioned, the bottom line is "that the human mind is prepared for tribalism."[3] So Paul declared that this segregating *conduct was not in step with the truth of the gospel.* The remainder of the letter was written to counteract this fault by exposing how harmful it is (5:19–21), and by exhibiting the potent beauty of justification in Christ Jesus, and how justification works out and works into our relationships and churches turning ethnic superiority on its head, along with other practices (3:26–29; 5:22–25).

Therefore the "works of the flesh" encompass a wide spectrum of sins and sinful tendencies, many of which promote assimilation-or-apartness: enmity, strife, fits of anger, dissensions, divisions, "and things like these." Returning racism to the range of actions listed under "the flesh" does several things. For starters, when we are tempted to point out other people's prejudices, we can humbly recognize that our own favorite sins are marching in lockstep with the other person's proclivities. We come to perceive that the category "works of the flesh" is like that laundry basket filled with our soiled linen.

Further, by keeping "racism" inside the works of the flesh, it is no longer narrowed down to a twentieth and twenty-first century class struggle but is shown to be something every Christian throughout the ages must address in themselves. We're in this together, and we all need God's help with this issue together, since:

In Christ Jesus you are all sons of God, through faith. For as many of you as were baptized into Christ have put on Christ. There is neither Jew nor Greek, there is neither slave nor free, there is no male and female, for you are all one in Christ Jesus. And if you are Christ's, then you are Abraham's offspring, heirs according to promise. (Gal. 3:26–29)

Also, it moves us away from depending on fashionable secular remedies, or modern-day pluralistic resolutions. Keeping "racism" in the spectrum of "flesh" reminds us that we've been here before. Its one of the reasons Paul wrote Galatians, Ephesians, Romans, etc. And if we've been here before, then we are not here alone. Over the last two thousand years, there have been several moments where this sin has been properly handled and times when it has been mishandled, and we can learn from those who have gone before us. And we can also take up a stance of humility. As Christopher Hutchinson observes:

> Regarding the past, believers look with horror upon the sins of slavery and Jim Crow, and rightly condemn both institutions. But do they really think that many believers today would have avoided the cultural pressures that captured so much of the church at that time? Would most of today's white Christians really have been among that small, persecuted minority in the antebellum American South who actively opposed slavery? (...) When today's believers evaluate the sins of past generations, humility and empathy are always in good order, even as they speak the truth and hold to the standards of God's Word. Christians might also consider what future generations will say about today's church when believers look back at our cultural accommodations. All have sinned and fallen short of the glory of God.[4]

Additionally, as we return "racism" to the "works of the flesh," we place our prejudices, and locate our congregations and denominations, back into the rocky, rearing rodeo called "sanctification." In this biblical framework of sanctification, we find that:

> The work of God's free grace, whereby we are renewed in the whole person (both individually and collectively) after the image of God, and are enabled more and more to die unto sin, and live unto righteousness.[5]

This work of sanctification is still being applied to us by God. Since these racial biases are part of the works of the flesh, which God is amending through his Spirit's actions in us, we become freed from faddish, state-of-the-art resolutions that are divorced from any recognition of total depravity and expect heaven-on-earth in our time and by our machinations. We become liberated to be freshly charitable and patient, knowing that ultimately the satisfying conclusion to the works of the flesh will finally come at Christ's return when in the fullness of time the Father will "unite all things in Christ, things in heaven and things on earth" (Eph. 1:10). All of these thoughts bring me to this final observation.

One New Man

When we approach "racism" as somewhere inside the realm of "the works of the flesh" we are given a new imagery and narrative. In Ephesians 2, Paul is again challenging the assimilation-or-apartness divide. And there he brings it to the cross in a similar though slightly different way:

> But now in Christ Jesus you who once were far off have been brought near by the blood of Christ. For he himself is our peace, who has made us both one and has broken down in his flesh the dividing wall of hostility..., that he might create in himself one new man (hena kainon anthropon) in place of the two, so making peace, and might reconcile us both to God in one body through the cross, thereby killing the hostility. (Eph. 2:13–16)

Christ's redemptive work draws together disparate ancestral and social groups to Christ giving us a whole new way of being human—together we become *one new man*. Paul plays this out a little later when he calls on the Christians:

> *To put off your old self* (ton palaion anthropon), *which belongs to your former manner of life and is corrupt through deceitful desires, and to be renewed in the spirit of your minds, and to put on the new self* (ton kainon anthropon), *created after the likeness of God in true righteousness and holiness.* (Eph. 4:22–24)

Part of our redeemed vocation is to strip ourselves of the old way of being human (*the old man*, Eph. 4:22), that old way that fleshes out ethnic bigotries as well as falsehood, stealing, corrupting talk, bitterness, wrath, anger, clamor, slander, malice, and unforgiveness (Eph. 4:25–32). Instead, we're to live on into another direction, to live out a whole new way of being human —*the new man*—together.

The new cross-shaped, Christ-bought imagery and narrative is that together in Christ, we are part of Christ's new way of being human; we are engrafted into his new humanity (*the new man* and *the one new man*), which gives us a new identity together and a new way of interacting and engaging with each other together. It liberates us from our old way of being human (*palaion anthropon*), with its vindictiveness and viciousness, egocentricity, and ethno-centricity. Being raised together with Christ and seated together with him in the heavenly places (Eph. 2:5), we are beginning to be what we will one day be completely, a new humankind!

The Sober Mind

None of this is to devalue the untold number of lynchings, cross-burnings, abuses, and violent actions. What it does do is it does point out to us what Aleksandr Solzhenitsyn correctly observed when he remarked:

> If only there were evil people somewhere insidiously committing evil deeds, and it were necessary only to separate them from the rest of us and destroy them. But the line dividing good and evil cuts through the heart of every human being. And who is willing to destroy a piece of his own heart?[6]

Scripture implicates each of us. And if, as in Plato's tale in *The Republic*, we could find the Ring of Gyges and become invisible and thus remain unaccountable for our actions, we would quickly find that the horrors we despise in others are swelling up from our own hearts.

Therefore, how does restoring the concept of "racism" back into the category of the "flesh" aid sober mindedness? First, if it helps us at all, it does so by removing our defensiveness. We find the seeds of envy, hate, bigotry, and violence already at work in our hearts. We can recognize that the itch of superiority, snobbishness, and sanctimonious smugness keeps on popping up its foul and fiendish head in our hearts. We come to acknowledge that there are times we are convinced that we're better than "them." This came home to me, years ago, in a way that I have since termed "The Six-Pack-More Rule." Let me explain.

I once received some intensive drug and alcohol abuse training while I was in the Air Force. It lasted about thirty days, and I learned quite a bit about how chemical abusers think and reason. It was an enlightening time and gave me plenty to reflect on.

After a period of training and instruction I was finally allowed to do an alcohol abuse intake on a young airman who had just come out of the hospital for alcohol poisoning. He had ingested so much beer in a short period of time that his liver shut down and he went into shock. Two days later, he was back on his feet and sitting before me.

As I interviewed him regarding his history, family, and drinking patterns, I asked how much he normally drank in a day. "Oh, about two six-packs a night," he replied, and he had been doing so for a year or more. "Did you say two six-packs a night, as in twelve whole bottles of beer?" He responded in the affirmative. So, I asked the next question, "Would you consider that you might be an alcoholic?" He scoffed and said, "Oh no, not me."

Then I backed up and came in a little lower, "Is it possible you would at least consider that you have a drinking problem?" Again, he strongly held out with a "No way!" Finally, I asked, "Can you think of someone you know whom you are certain has a drinking problem? And if so, how much do they drink?" He surprised me with his answer, "Oh, yes. That would be my friend Joe. He drinks a six-pack more than me."

The six-pack-more rule reasons that I'm okay because I'm better than that guy or gal over there. I've seen this played out between ex-convicts, as well as prostitutes and sexually promiscuous people. And have seen it in "normal," upstanding, law-abiding folks. Comparing ourselves to others so that we're on the "I'm better than they are" side.

But when we come to grasp how "the works of the flesh" are in us, no matter our ancestry, ethnicity, political party, neighborhood, net worth, or educational attainments, then it helps us have our heads on straight. It gives us the ability to set aside our defensiveness. And we're no longer startled that we, and others, have trouble trusting and working with people who are not like us.

It gives us a healthier insight into Tutsis rampaging and ravaging and murdering hundreds of thousands of Hutus, fellow Africans. We can fathom why Japanese, Koreans, and Chinese struggle with dislike for one another. We become sensitive to the ways Kiowas, Comanches, Apaches, Tonkawas, and other First

Nation peoples, see themselves as different from each other, and maybe better than each other. And we are enabled to come to grips with the way each of us, no matter our descent or ethnicity, are part of the problem in the United States of America, and more importantly, inside God's church. Bigotry in America and American churches is not dichromatic, black-and-white. Rather, it is the bleak outworking of fallen humankind. But now, no longer stumbling into the rut of the old imagery and narrative that gets us off the hook, we are wisened to our own inner "six-pack-more rule."

And yet, we are presented with hopefulness. Now, with clear heads unencumbered by the old imagery and narrative, and able to see that the works of the flesh are universal, we run to Christ, who in his incarnation, death, burial, resurrection, and ascension, has launched our new way of being human. That in the one man, Jesus Christ, the grace of God and the free gift of grace by that man abounds to many no matter their ancestry, ethnicity, or descent (Rom. 5:15). Now we can begin putting aside the old way of being human with its bigotry, arrogance, ethnocentricity, and violence. We are able to take on a whole new way of being human.

Declared righteous before God by the righteousness of Jesus, despite what we deserve, we can embrace others declared righteous, even, and especially, those who are different from us. We can risk acknowledging "the works of the flesh" in us, and we can see a way forward through the one who has been lifted up and is drawing all people to himself (John 12:32). No longer bound to the disorienting and distressing imagery and narrative that fuels defensiveness, derision, callous indifference, excuse-making that rationalizes away responsibility, we can see how we have been part of the disease and can begin to be part of the remedy. Truly, the grace of God trains us *"to renounce ungodliness and worldly passions, and to live self-controlled* (sophronos), *upright, and godly lives in the present age"* (Titus 2:12).

1. Ta-Nehisi Coates, "Playing the Racist Card."
2. Though Paul does momentarily attend upon one set of sexual immoralities, he does so as an example, and then quickly launches into a pile of other immoral actions. He continues doing this through chapters 2–3 to bring his readers to acknowledge that there's none righteous, no not one (3:10ff).
3. Greg Lukianoff and Jonathan Haidt, *The Coddling of the American Mind*, 58.
4. Hutchinson, Op. Cit., 204–5.
5. Westminster Shorter Catechism, Question and Answer 35
6. Aleksandr I. Solzhenitsyn, *The Gulag Archipelago*, Translated by Thomas P. Whitney, (New York: Harper & Row Publishers, 1974), 168.

TRUE WITNESS

Vital though presidents and governments are,
relationships matter more to freedom than regimes.
The personal and the interpersonal precede the political.

—Os Guinness, *Last Call for Liberty*

He was at the top of his cycling game. He secured seven Tour de France titles, and his success was such that he had earned the respect of many and was able to guide the rules for competitive cycling. And then it all came tumbling down. Years of doping but worse—lying and covering it up. Probably the one thing that ticks us off the most about this famous cyclist is the bald-faced lying. The verbal and physical swaggering as he looked squarely into the camera while he repeatedly denied any use of performance enhancing drugs. And now, after months upon months and years upon years of this, there was an admission of guilt. He lied to his fans.

Lying is a form of giving false testimony, speaking falsehoods to and about others. And the liberating God of Truth has something to say to these things in what most Protestants call the

Ninth Commandment.[1] As we continue to think through what it means to be sober-minded, it will be worth our time to plunge into God's directive that we not bear false witness against our neighbor (Exod. 20:16; Deut. 5:20).

Before we head deep into the commandment, there are three items to take note of. To begin, the Ten Commandments, or the Decalogue, flow out of God's grace and redemption. These instructions do not begin with the first directive but with Yahweh's liberating love: *"I am the LORD your God, who brought you out of the land of Egypt, out of the house of slavery"* (Exod. 20:2, and Deut. 5:6). It's as if Yahweh is saying, "I'm the God who set you free. Now here's how free people live free."

Further, the commandments are in the second person singular. Even though all of Israel is gathered en masse at the foot of the mountain, Yahweh addresses each individual Miriam, Elisheba, Eleazer and Ithamar assembled. To every man, woman, girl and boy, God says *"I have freed you,… therefore, you shall… and you shall not…."*

Finally, the One who says we should not bear false witness against our neighbor does not appear to be giving a carte blanche, absolute prohibition to all untruth. For example, later he guides Nathan to use fiction to teach David a lesson (2 Sam. 12). And Yahweh also directs the use of deceit in military actions, such as in Joshua 8.

What is Yahweh after in this commandment?

The Obvious Is Obvious

Clearly, and at the primary level, this is a proscription against perjury in a judicial setting. Toward the goal of fostering truthfulness in law, Yahweh will later set up the need for multiple witnesses who can corroborate the facts of the situation. Therefore:

> A single witness shall not suffice against a person for any crime or for any wrong in connection with any offense that he has committed. Only on the evidence of two witnesses or of three witnesses shall a charge be established. If a malicious witness arises to accuse a person of wrongdoing, then both parties to the dispute shall appear before the Lord, before the priests and the judges who are in office in those days. The judges shall inquire diligently, and if the witness is a false witness and has accused his brother falsely, then you shall do to him as he had meant to do to his brother. (Deut. 19:15–19).

The same pattern of checks and balances applies in the church regarding congregational leaders: *"Do not admit a charge against an elder except on the evidence of two or three witnesses"* (1 Tim. 5:19). And it applies when one Christian accuses another of wrongdoing who persists in denying any wrong done: *"But if he does not listen, take one or two others along with you, that every charge may be established by the evidence of two or three witnesses"* (Matt. 18:16) The breadth of the commandment is evident. It applies to witnesses and lawyers, elders and congregations.

The liberating God wants his people to remain free shows, and that liberty relies heavily on the freedom from being slandered, from having one's reputation slaughtered and smeared. As the Westminster Shorter Catechism states, the Ninth Commandment requires we maintain and promote truth between people, as well as the integrity of our own and our neighbor's good name, most especially in witness-bearing.[2]

And it forbids whatever is prejudicial to truth or harms and damages our own or our neighbor's good name. And as Luther's Small Catechism explains, we should fear and love God in such a way that we refuse to tell lies about our neighbors, or betray them, slander them, or harm their reputation. Instead, we are expected to defend our neighbors, speaking well of them, and do the best we can to explain their actions and intents in the kindest way.[3]

The principle, then, invites us to take it further. Most certainly the liberating God's freedom-loving injunction applies to the realm of radio programs, podcasts, and TV talk show hosts, especially in the way they present condemning "evidence" and accusations about presidents, politicians, pastors, and people. Even if a broadcaster is convinced that their cause is right and their ratings need to be bolstered, it doesn't give him or her permission to bear false testimony about others. And part of giving false testimony includes telling only part of the truth while leaving out the portion of facts and evidence that would change the story. This applies as well to Christian anchors when they talk about other Christians: *"Therefore, having put away falsehood, let each one of you speak the truth with his neighbor, for we are members one of another"* (Eph. 5:25).

Without a doubt, the freeing God's way to help us remain free includes what we do regarding gossip, tale bearing, and smearing someone's reputation, whether it's by word of mouth, email, social media, or blogs. For example, several years back, I received an email from someone I've known for years. This person didn't like the sitting president and was worried that the administration was destroying the country. So, this person forwarded a chain-email that condemned the president for an executive order, giving supposed evidence that the executive order funded American enemies.

I did my research and found that the accusation was true to an extent, while leaving out two facts: 1) other presidents (both Republican and Democrat) had signed the same executive order before him; and 2) the funding was actually part of a long-term American policy of winning friends by aiding elementary and secondary schools inside the region of our foes.

Whether one agrees with the wisdom of the executive order or not, it wasn't a clandestine action to sabotage American interests. I pointed out to this person that even if they didn't like the president, and they wished this email were true so they could continue to suspect and accuse him, we Christians have a clear obligation—out of love for our liberating God and out of love for liberty—to not pass on something that bore false testimony, no matter how true we want it to be.

Most pointedly, this is the case for Christians speaking or posting or publishing about other Christians. As the Apostle Paul notes:

> *Do not lie to one another, seeing that you have put off the old self with its practices and have put on the new self, which is being renewed in knowledge after the image of its creator. Here there is not Greek and Jew, circumcised and uncircumcised, barbarian, Scythian, slave, free; but Christ is all, and in all.* (Col. 3:9–11)

As we saw in a previous chapter, since we have been united to Christ we have put off the old way of being human (*ton palaion anthropon*), and we have put on the new way of being human (*ton neon anthropon*), So we are to put away lying and be truth tellers to and about one another because Christ is all and in all. On this last statement, Samuel Logan has rightly noticed that:

> When we say anything about other professed Christians, the total content of our remarks—both denotation and connotation—gets applied, whether we intend it or not, to him whose name we share.[4]

Since all Christians bear the name of Christ, as is made clear in our baptism and confession of faith (Matt. 28:19; Rom. 10:9–10), then, if we slander or slur a fellow believer, we are casting shame on the name of our Lord. In other words, we become party to those who take the Lord's name in vain.

Lying Lives Deep

Lying goes deep into our being and fallen nature. It began in the Garden (Gen. 3), and it goes to the end of time as we know it. It originates with the Devil (the slanderer). In John, Jesus says:

You are of your father the devil, and your will is to do your father's desires. He was a murderer from the beginning, and does not stand in the truth, because there is no truth in him. When he lies, he speaks out of his own character, for he is a liar and the father of lies. (John 8:44)

And in a way, you can say we ourselves become hell-bent on lying. James writes:

And the tongue is a fire, a world of unrighteousness. The tongue is set among our members, staining the whole body, setting on fire the entire course of life, and set on fire by hell. (James 3:6)

We exchange the truth about God for lies (Rom. 1:25). And as humans go deeper into wretchedness, at some point God himself gives them up to deception:

Because they refused to love the truth and so be saved. Therefore God sends them a strong delusion, so that they may believe what is false, in order that all may be condemned who did not believe the truth but had pleasure in unrighteousness. (2 Thess. 2:10b–12).

There are times when even highly religious people desire ministers, shamans, prophets, and prognosticators to go on affirming us in our deceptions. Paul writes:

For the time is coming when people will not endure sound teaching, but having itching ears they will accumulate for themselves teachers to suit their own passions, and will turn away from listening to the truth and wander off into myths. (2 Tim. 4:3–4)

If we can dare to be honest, we're in it up to our ears; lying lives deep!

The World in the World and the World in the Church

Greg Lukianoff, president and CEO of the Foundation for Individual Rights in Education, and Jonathan Haidt, the Thomas Cooley professor of Ethical Leadership at New York University's Stern School of Business, teamed up in 2018 to assess and analyze troubles they have seen brewing in Academia and American society. They compiled their insights into 352 pages entitled *The Coddling of the American Mind: How Good Intentions and Bad Ideas are Setting Up a Generation for Failure.*

They deal with three damaging myths that have been grabbing hold of academia, students, and beyond. The harmful triumvirate began showing their colors on campuses around 2013 and have been spilling into society. The three untruths are: 1) What doesn't kill you makes you weaker (fragility); 2) Always trust your feelings (emotional reasoning); and 3) Life is a battle between good people and evil people (us versus them).

Lukianoff and Haidt masterfully show:

How these three Great Untruths—and the policies and political movements that draw on them—are causing problems for young people, universities, and, more generally, liberal democracies.[5]

From this mendacious trifecta has arisen a growing, harmful, sense of fragility, the need for safe spaces, the concept of microaggressions, increasing cognitive distortions, the taking up common-enemy identity politics, and the shaming trend of a call-out culture—to name a few of the troubles. Most people are familiar with a call-out culture on social media, which includes grandstanding and "virtue signaling" where people say and do things to publicize that they are virtuous. This helps them to stay in the inner ring of their virtual posse. The result is the rise of mob-mentality. The authors then observe that mobs:

> Can rob good people of their conscience, particularly when participants wear masks (in a real mob) or are hiding behind an alias or avatar (in an online mob). Anonymity fosters disindividuation—the loss of an individual sense of self—which lessens self-restraint and increases one's willingness to go along with the mob.[6]

Here is the world in the world, the growing fragmentation of community and society, polarized and pulled apart into mobs and factions. These divisions progressively "other" those they disagree with, demanding a form of political correctness—whether conservative or liberal, right or left—and damning those that are outside the tribe. The result is a mindset that others are guilty until proven innocent. And this world in the world has been leaking into the church.

It doesn't take much reflection to see how the world that has been infecting the world is now the world infecting the church. An easy mark is the grandstanding and virtue signaling, which arises from most crews, whether they are identified as "conservatives" or "social justice warriors." But more simply, listen for the "guilty until proven innocent" concept within the pious perimeters of Christian circles. This is more than the old family rivalries and ribbings between denominations. There is a growing disinterest in listening to and hearing what other Christians are actually saying, and immediately jumping to conclusions of guilt first, calling out the "guilty" and often times misreading and mishearing what they have written or said. We now say things online we would rarely say to someone eyeball-to-eyeball.

Psychologists are calling these actions the "online disinhibition effect." It is where social inhibitions decrease, and we say things that if we were in our right minds, we wouldn't say—as when someone is becoming inebriated. This is the world in the world, and it is now the world in the church.

In Our Right Minds

Since, as *"God gave us a spirit not of fear but of power and love and self-control (sophronismou)"* and since the grace of God trains us *"to renounce ungodliness and worldly passions, and to live self-controlled (sophronos), upright, and godly lives in the present age"* (2 Tim. 1:7; Titus 2:12), then we have a clear indication of where to go so we can be in our right minds. It is to our great God and Savior, Jesus Christ:

> *Who gave himself for us to redeem us from all lawlessness (which includes bearing false witness) and to purify for himself a people for his own possession who are zealous for good works.* (Titus 2:14)

It is to Jesus Christ, who is the way, the truth, the life, and the only way to the Father (John 14:6). It is to the One who encompasses truth (Eph. 4:21).

Then, as we turn—or return—to Jesus, we must confess our sins in this area. We are promised, *"If we confess our sins, he is faithful and just to forgive us our sins and to cleanse us from all unrighteousness"* (1 John 1:9). In dealing with this topic, and working through Samuel Logan's book referenced above, I found myself doing just that. Here is the confession of sin I penned as I worked through this commandment. Maybe you can use it:

> I implore you, O God of truth, to grant me wisdom, strength, and a sober mind that I would not give into whatever is prejudicial to truth, or injurious to my own or my neighbor's good name.

Rather, that I would maintain and promote truth between man and man, as well as my own and my neighbor's good name (Westminster Shorter Catechism 77, 78). Lord, it is all too easy to give into my own sourness, self-promotion, or fear of failure, and to speak from there. But it is what comes out of the mouth that defiles me, for it proceeds from my heart. For out of my heart comes evil thoughts, murder, adultery, sexual immorality, theft, false witness and slander (Matt. 15.18– 20). Good God! Have mercy on me, forgive me, and change me. Amen.

Next, after coming to Jesus and confessing our sin of bearing false witness, we then put off false testimony and put on truth. This requires we remember that the good name of Jesus ought to be the aim of our lives and lips (the Third Commandment, to not take or bear God's name in vain, still applies, too). It also necessitates that we acknowledge God alone has unfailing knowledge of the other person's heart, motives, intentions, and condition. Thus, we should be humble in our assessments, and charitable in our evaluations of other people. Even Lukianoff and Haidt see the value of being charitable in our disagreements and discussions, as they observe that there:

Is a principle in philosophy and rhetoric called the principle of charity, which says that one should interpret other people's statements in their best, most reasonable form, not in the worst or most offensive way possible.[7]

Further, we must put to the side labels, those short-hand terms we use to describe others, since most of them are derogatory and often do not promote truth-telling or honorable disagreements and discussions. And we should refrain from relying on social media posts and tweets to win points.

I find it convicting and humbling that many voices outside of the church are speaking on this very topic. Recently, Jonathan

Haidt and Tobias Rose-Stockwell have addressed the factionalism raging in our country, and I would add our churches, and how social media has made it too easy. They write:

> As social media has aged, however, optimism has faded and the list of known or suspected harms has grown: Online political discussions (often among anonymous strangers) are experienced as angrier and less civil than those in real life; networks of partisans co-create worldviews that can become more and more extreme; disinformation campaigns flourish; violent ideologies lure recruits.[8]

They go on to analyze the reasons behind the trouble, addressing the moral grandstanding that demands—without historical context or ancestral wisdom—that readers must side with this faction or that party right this minute. These are platforms that make outrage contagious. The authors end with their suggestions for remediation, which are a start.

One way we can be part of the cure rather than the disease is to be a people who are in our right minds, not giving out partial truth, nor giving in to untruth. Another way to say it is—to have our heads on right, we are not stepping onto the platforms of contagious outrage. Because Jesus has made the church *"the household of God, which is the church of the living God, a pillar and buttress of the truth"* (1 Tim. 3:15), truth-telling and truthful witness should be a priority in our congregations and from our churches. That is, truth-telling from the stance of charity.

Whether it's about the congregation's leadership (1 Tim. 5:17–20), the character of fellow parishioners, political actions, or social events, our aim ought to be to give truthful testimony in a way that interprets actions and statements in their best, most reasonable form rather than in the worst and most damning way possible. We stand in the long, biblical tradition of innocent until proven guilty. In a world that seems to be in a love affair with half-truths, alt-truth, fake truths, character assaults, guilty until proven innocent, steamy and salacious stories, etc.—all which are platforms for making outrage contagious—part of our being sober minded is being a truthful people. And especially truthful toward, and truthful with regard to, all who call upon the name of the Lord Jesus Christ, "both their Lord and ours" (1 Cor. 1:2).

There is more that could be written on the Ninth Commandment and the importance of caring about our own and our neighbor's good name. Thankfully a book has been published recently by Samuel T. Logan, Jr. entitled *The Good Name: The Power of Words to Hurt and Heal*. It thoughtfully gives more detail, and I highly recommend it.[9]

---

1. Some Lutherans and Anglicans number it as the Eighth Commandment, as do the Catholic and Orthodox traditions.
2. Westminster Shorter Catechism, Question and Answer 77, 78.
3. Concordia Publishing House, *Luther's Small Catechism*.
4. Samuel T. Logan, Jr., *The Good Name*, 44.
5. Lukianoff and Haidt, Op. Cit., 4.
6. Ibid., 73.
7. Ibid., 55.
8. Jonathan Haidt and Tobias Rose-Stockwell, *The Dark Psychology of Social Networks*."
9. Logan, Op. Cit., 73–102.

EAGLE'S WINGS

Those that are the objects of God's preserving
care can never fail to reach the desired end;
for through the means which that loving care provides,
they patiently persevere until they inherit the kingdom.

—Charles Octavius Boothe, *Plain Theology for Plain People*

Adults and kids do this. For example, when your supervisor calls you on the carpet for muffing a project, or failing to meet some major deadline, we respond, "Yes boss. I know." Or after the police officer pulls you over and tells you you've been doing fifty in a school zone, you respond, "Yes, officer. I know. I know." And when parents start telling kids how to do this chore properly or that task more efficiently, they almost always reply, "I know."

It's funny, we "know," but our mistake or misstep shows that at another level we didn't "know" because if we really did, we wouldn't have done it that poorly or forgotten to do it. This tension between "I know. I know" and "knowing" runs right through the Bible like an artery, and in Isaiah 40:27–31 the "blue vein" of genuine "knowing" is just visible beneath the skin.

Questions

The Bible is full of questions. Many people in the Bible are asking God questions like "How long, O LORD?" or "Why do you hide your face?" But the Bible also has questions from God to us.

Here are two questions that God is asking in 40:28: "Have you not known? Have you not heard?" These are reflecting and probing questions meant to make us all stop and ruminate. These are questions that challenge us with "Have you not known certain things about God." The whole chapter is full of these queries.

- v. 12: *"Who has measured the waters in the hollow of his hand?"*
- v. 14: *"Who taught God the path of justice?"*
- v. 18: *"To whom will you liken God?"*
- v. 21: *"Do you not know? Do you not hear?"*
- v. 25: *"To whom will you compare me?"*

When the Bible records God asking questions, especially in a setting like this, it's always good to stop, take a deep breath and reflect: "Have I not known certain things about God?!"

God

Yahweh is asking us about what we really know. Have you not known and heard that God is everlasting and eternal? Have you not known and heard that God is the Creator of the ends of the earth? Have you not known and heard that this God never weakens, faints, or gets weary, but instead his understanding is unsearchable? Or that he is the one who gives power to those collapsing, increasing strength to those who are powerless?

This is the God we are being asked to reflect on—who he is and what he does for his people. At this point, we realize we're supposed to nod our heads in pious assent, say "Amen," or mumble something like, "Why sure enough; in fact, who doesn't know all of these things?!"

But do you *really* know? Is there a certainty and assurance in your heart, or are there dark, dank, dreary doubts and question marks bubbling up from the deep places of your being?

Disappointments

There is disappointment lurking here (40:27). So God, through the prophet, is addressing the reason for the disappointment by bringing up examples of what we normally are impressed with: strength and energy! And he specifically mentions those whom we assume or think are energy-driven, power-packed, high-octane, ever-ready-bunny kind of people—youth!

We almost always think of young people, kids, and teens as being inexhaustible and boundless in their energy and that there's no off button anywhere, so they just go and go. But even they will run out of gas, get exhausted, tired, and peter out (40:30). And when this verse is placed next to the description of Yahweh in verses 28–29, we see the point. It is this God *alone* who never wears out, who never gets tuckered out, who never falls out exhausted. Everything else we think is powerful, full of resources, beefed up with unstoppable strength—whether super football players, nuclear energy, petroleum, the sun, or whatever—all of these will run out of fuel at some point, deflate and fall flat.

But not this God! Is it possible we are disappointed because we have been impressed with the wrong things?

Hope

Now, who is it in 40:31 that ends up being renewed in strength, recharged, running, and not getting weary or faint? It is those who wait for the inexhaustible Yahweh. In the Hebrew, the word carries the idea of those who await with hope, those who have an expectant, patient trust. When we're out of gas—empty, broken, exhausted, weak, spent—it's the God of Abraham, Isaac, and Jacob who rises up to catch us and make us able, even when we're no longer normally or naturally able, and he carries us along with himself.

Commentator J. Alec Motyer looks at the contrast going on here in verses 30 and 31, and he remarks:

> The natural person (30a) is not like God (28e) but the believer is, as the unwearying, unfainting strength of the divine enters him he finds inner resources that do not fail before life's demands.[1]

This passage also gives us an interesting description of what God does here. He is pictured as an eagle swooping up and catching those falling. This is like Tolkien's description in *The Hobbit* when Gandalf and the dwarves are at the end of the tree that is falling over the cliff, and they start tumbling down through the air. Suddenly, unlooked for, up swoops the eagles to catch them. It's the same kind of picture here because that's what our rescuing God is like.

This eagle picture for Yahweh is used in another place. When God had rescued his people from Egypt—saving those who could not save themselves and liberating those who could not liberate themselves—he describes his liberating-rescuing-saving action in eagle-terms: *"You yourselves have seen what I did to the Egyptians, and how I bore you on eagles' wings and brought you to myself"* (Exod. 19:4). His rescue of his people—liberating and emancipating them—is pictured like an eagle swooping in to save them and bear them away to the only place of safety, to himself.

That is what Jesus did, by dying on the cross for his people and rising again on the third day:

> *Our great God and Savior Jesus Christ, who gave himself for us to redeem us from all lawlessness and to purify for himself a people for his own possession who are zealous for good works.* (Titus 2:13c–14)

In his death and resurrection, our Lord Jesus rises up like a rescuing eagle to retrieve-recover-redeem-emancipate us and bear us to safety, to bring us to himself. Isaiah writes:

> *Even youths shall faint and be weary, and young men shall fall exhausted; but they who wait for the LORD shall renew their strength; they shall mount up with wings like eagles; they shall run and not be weary; they shall walk and not faint.* (Isa. 40:30–31)

Because the grace of God is *"training us to renounce ungodliness and worldly passions, and to live self-controlled* (sophronos), *upright, and godly lives in the present age"* (Titus 2:12), this passage is helpful for us in getting our heads on straight. In the face of the discouraging let-downs and loads of disappointments, it's good to ask: "Where have I been placing my confidences? Have I been impressed with all the wrong things? Have I been enthralled in my own engineered know-how or muscle? Have I been fascinated by my own vitality or vanity? If so, Yahweh invites us, you and me, to come to our right minds regarding our endurance and to turn our faces up to him.

Further, as you ponder and reflect on the things you should know about this God, it is fitting to go down deeper. Plunge beneath the pious head nodding and to start looking, asking, and researching your heart: "Am I in the "I Know I know" place, or do I really know this God?"

It's possible that some reading this volume are presently in free-fall, with arms flailing, legs kicking, and torsos wriggling in mid-air as you feel like you're plummeting. Maybe you're in the middle time of your life, and there are creeping disappointments or disenchantments with your parenting or career. Possibly the flight path you're on right now was nowhere in your plans. Maybe you're a young adult and the load you're under is choking and stifling. Maybe you're in the later years of your life, where the number of your friends are starting to thin-out numerically, and your body (and perchance your mind) are beginning to feel like they are withering, and you're sensing a purposelessness.

Wherever you are, it is likely starting to feel as if your roller-coaster has derailed now that you've crested the top of the track! Free fall! Think of how odd it would be if at this moment you say to God: "Hey, no problem. I've got this! I'll figure this one out on my own. Thanks, but no thanks!"

Part of being in our right mind includes casting aside the supposed self-sufficiency and latching on to the One who took the doom and bad karma of his people, slaughtered it in his death on the cross, and was raised from the dead on the third day. The One who rises up as a rescuing eagle that he may bring you to himself. The One who will renew your strength; who will mount you up with wings like eagles; who will make you able to run and not be weary; to walk and not faint.

Surely, throwing yourself on him is the very heart of being in your right mind:

> Even youths shall faint and be weary, and young men shall fall exhausted; but they who wait for the LORD shall renew their strength; they shall mount up with wings like eagles; they shall run and not be weary; they shall walk and not faint. (Isa. 40:30–31)
>
> For God gave us a spirit not of fear but of power and love and self-control (2 Tim. 1:7)

He was standing before a local magistrate and two dignitaries to defend himself from accusations leveled at him by powerful elites. As he spoke, he recounted his violent background and vicious account. And then he explained where it all changed in his Damascus-road experience. Jesus changed his whole life. Jesus had cut him off, closed him down, caught him up, and cast him into a new mold. And it was at just the moment of rehearsing his tale that the magistrate charged him with mania:

> *And as he was saying these things in his defense, Festus said with a loud voice, "Paul, you are out of your mind* (mainia); *your great learning is driving you out of your mind* (manian)." *But Paul said: "I am not out of my mind* (mainomai), *most excellent Festus, but I am speaking true* (alatheias) *and rational* (sophrosunas) *words. For the king knows about these things, and to him I speak boldly. For I am persuaded that none of these things has escaped his notice, for this has not been done in a corner.* (Acts 26:24–26)

Mania versus right-mindedness.

Several years later, Paul was writing to a church he had planted. Some were accusing him of being a bit off, even to the point of doubting that he was one of Jesus' handpicked spokesmen. In his second letter to these Christians, he stated in one of his defenses:

> *For if we are beside ourselves* (exestemen), *it is for God; if we are in our right mind* (sophronoumen), *it is for you. For the love of Christ controls us, because we have concluded this: that one has died for all, therefore all have died; and he died for all, that those who live might no longer live for themselves but for him who for their sake died and was raised.* (2 Cor. 5:13–15)

Ecstasy versus right-mindedness.

In these two snippets, we find ourselves right back where we began in Mark 4:35–5:20—the contrast between being out of our minds and being in our right minds. And the way of right-mindedness is found the 2 Corinthians 5:14: *"For the love of Christ controls us."* The challenge is this—will we be beside ourselves and caught up in mania, or will we be controlled by the love of Christ in sober-mindedness.

This short book has been my earnest endeavor to think through more thoroughly a subject I have been pondering since the 1980s while I was in Air Force. Those old "Friends of Bill" gave me some helpful classifications that have been useful over the years. Whether my analysis garners your complete agreement or not, it is evident that sobriety, having a sober mind, is a valuable biblical virtue. It is a virtue grounded in the Gospel and grace of our great God and Savior Jesus Christ, and it affects our lives, perspectives, and relationships.

---

1. J. Alec Motyer, *The Prophecy of Isaiah*, 308.

AFTERWORD

Where would I like to see things go from here for God's people and especially readers of this volume?

Simply, that we would be known by our society as a people who have their heads on straight. I'm not concerned that American culture likes us or agrees with us. But I am eager for us to be steady and stable, not given over to whatever alarmist wave comes washing through to sweep us off our feet. I want us to learn and practice better what it means to not be overcome by evil but to overcome evil with good (Rom. 12:21). Also, I am keen on our presenting before the eyes of our watching world lifestyles that keep the word of God from being reviled and don't allow the opponent to have anything evil to say of us. May we have habits and lives that in every way adorn the doctrine of God our Savior (Titus 2:5, 8, 10). And last, I am hopeful that working through this book will bring all of us to a deeper, richer trust in our storm-calming Savior and squall-conquering Sovereign.

Dare I hope it? Is it possible that reading through this manuscript can bring us to lift our hearts and voices to sing with the ancient church?

Praise the Savior now and ever;
praise him, all beneath the skies;
prostrate lying, suff'ring,
dying on the cross, a sacrifice.
Vict'ry gaining, life obtaining,
now in glory he doth rise.

Man's work faileth, Christ's availeth;
he is all our righteousness;
he, our Savior, has forever set us free
from dire distress.
Through his merit we inherit
light and peace and happiness.

Sin's bonds severed, we're delivered;
Christ has bruised the serpent's head;
death no longer is the stronger;
hell itself is captive led.
Christ has risen from death's prison;
o'er the tomb he light has shed.

For his favor, praise for ever
unto God the Father sing;
praise the Savior, praise him ever,
Son of God, our Lord and King.
Praise the Spirit; through Christ's merit
he doth us salvation bring.[1]

Toward that end, I offer this prayer for us all:

Now may the God and Father of our Lord Jesus Christ, who has not given us a spirit of fear, but of power, love and sober-mindedness, grant us, by his molding, shaping grace, to renounce ungodliness and worldly lusts and to live soberly, righteously and godly in this present age as we longingly look for the glorious appearing of our Great God and Savior Jesus Christ, who gave himself for us to liberate us from all lawlessness and to purify us for himself as his own special treasure, a people zealous for good works. Amen.

---

1. Venantius H.C. Fortunatus, "Praise the Savior Now and Ever," 243.

WORKS CITED

The 5 Man Electrical Band, 1971, "Signs."

Ambrose, "O Splendor of God's Glory Bright," In *Trinity Hymnal, Rev. Ed.*, (Atlanta-Philadelphia: Great Commission Publications).

The Anglican Church in North America, *The Book of Common Prayer*, (Huntington Beach: Anglican Liturgy Press, 2019).

The Apostolic Fathers Vol. 1, Edited by Bart D. Ehrman, Translated by Bart D. Ehrman, (Cambridge: Harvard University Press, 2003).

Arthur Bennett, *The Valley of Vision*, "Peril," Edited by Arthur Bennett, (Carlisle: The Banner of Truth Trust).

Biography.com, "Robert Downey Jr. Biography," A&E Television Networks, April 27, 2017.

Charles Octavious Boothe, *Plain Theology for Plain People*, (Bellingham: Lexham Press, 2017 (1890)).

Geoffrey W. Bromiley, *Theological Dictionary of the New Testament: Abridged in One Volume*, (Grand Rapids: William B. Eerdmans Publishing Company, 1985).

Albert E. Brumley, "This World Is Not My Home," Public Domain.

Michelle Carr, "Dream Deprived: A Modern Epidemic?" *Psychology Today*, August 22, 2017, https://www.psychologytoday.com/us/blog/dream-factory/201708/dream-deprived-modern-epidemic.

Ta-Nehisi Coates, "Playing the Racist Card," *Slate*, March 14, 2008, https://slate.com/news-and-politics/2008/03/ferraro-s-comments-about-obama-were-racist-why-can-t-we-say-that.html

Concordia Publishing House, *Luther's Small Catechism*, 2019, https://catechism.cph.org/en/10-commandments.html.

Fanny J. Crosby, "All the Way My Savior Leads Me," In *Trinity Hymnal, Rev. Ed,* (Atlanta-Philadelphia: Great Commission Publications, 1990 (1875)).

Dale Ralph Davis, *1 Samuel: Looking on the Heart,* (Ross-shire: Christian Focus Publications, 2000 (1988)).

Sally Fitzgerald, *The Habit of Being: The Letters of Flannery O'Connor,* (New York: Farrar, Straus, Giroux, 1979).

Johann Franck, "Jesus, Priceless Treasure," In *Trinity Hymnal, Rev. Ed.,* 656, (Atlanta-Philadelphia: Great Commission Publications, 1990 (1655)).

Keith Getty and Stuart Townend, "In Christ Alone," (Brentwood: ThankYou Music LTD (Capitol CMG Publishing)).

Os Guinness, *Carpe Diem Redeemed: Seizing the Day, Discerning the Times,* (Downers Grove,: Intervarsity Press, 2019).

Os Guinness, *Last Call for Liberty,* (Downers Grove: InterVarsity Press, 2018).

Jonathan Haidt and Tobias Rose-Stockwell, "The Dark Psychology of Social Networks," *The Atlantic*, December2020, https://www.theatlantic.com/magazine/archive/2019/12/social-   media-democracy/600763.

Harvard Health Letter, "Sexually transmitted disease? At my age?"Edited by Harvard Medical School, 2018, https://www.health.harvard.edu/diseases-and-conditions/sexu- ally-transmitted-disease-at-my-age.

Christopher A. Hutchinson, *Rediscovering Humility*, (Greensboro: New Growth Press, 2018).

Carmen Joy Imes, *Bearing God's Name: Why Sinai Still Matters*, (Downers Grove: IVP Academic, 2020).

Kelly M. Kapic, *Embodied Hope*, (Downers Grove: IVP Academic, 2017).

Peter J. Leithart, *1 & 2 Kings*, (Grand Rapids: Baker Publishing Group, 2006).

Samuel T. Logan, Jr., *The Good Name: The Power of Words to Hurt or Heal*, (Greensboro: New Growth Press, 2019)

Loeb Classical Library, *The Apostolic Fathers Vol. 2*, Edited by Bart D. Erhman, (Cambridge: Harvard University Press, Loeb Classical Library).

Johannes P. Louw and Eugene P. Nida, *Greek-English Lexicon of the New Testament Based on Semantic Domains Second Edition*, Edited by Rondal B. Smith and Karen A. Munson. Vol. 1. 2 vols, (New York: United Bible Society).

Greg Lukianoff and Jonathan Haidt, *The Coddling of the American Mind*, (New York: Penguin Press, 2018).

Alice Marriott, *The Ten Grandmothers: Epic of the Kiowas*, (Norman: University of Oklahoma Press, 1945).

J. Alec Motyer, *The Prophecy of Isaiah*, (Downers Grove: InterVarsity Press, 1993).

Richard John Neuhaus, *American Babylon: Notes of a Christian Exile*, (New York: Basic Books, 2009).

John Newton, "Amazing Grace" In *Trinity Hymnal, Rev. Ed*, (Atlanta, Philadelphia: Great Commission Publications).

Northumbria Community, *Northumbria Community*, January 1, 2019, https://www.northumbriacommunity.org/offices/wednesday-the-felgild-compline/.

Dennis Okholm, *Dangerous Passions, Deadly Sins*, (Grand Rapids: Brazos Press, 2014).

Albrecht von Preussen, "The Will of God Is Always Best," In *Lutheran Service Book*, by The Commission on Worship of the Lutheran Church—Missouri Synod, (St. Louis: Concordia, 2006 (1554)).

Adraan Rademaker, *Sophrosyne and the Rhetoric of Self-Restraint*, (Leiden-Boston: Brill Academic Publishers, 2005).

John Roberts, "You Sons of the Gods." In *The Book of Psalms for Worship*, by The Board of Education and Publication of the Reformed Presbyterian Church of North America, (Pittsburgh: Crown and Covenant Publications, 2005).

Marilynne Robinson, "Fear," *New York Times Review of Books,* https://www.nybooks.com/articles/2015/09/24/marilynne-robinson-fear/.

Christine Rudisel and Bob Blaisdell, *Slave Narratives of the Underground Railroad,* (Mineola: Dover Publications, Inc., 2014).

Dorothy L. Sayers, *Christian Letters to a Post-Christian World: A Selection of Essays,* (Grand Rapids: Eerdmans, 1969).

Septuagint. *Elpenor,* https://www.ellopos.net/elpenor/greek-texts/septuagint/.

Andrew Solomon, *The Noonday Demon: An Atlas of Depression,* (New York: Scribner, 2001).

Aleksandr I. Solzhenitsyn, *The Gulag Archipelago,* Translated by Thomas P. Whitney, (New York: Harper & Row Publishers, 1974).

Tate and Brady, "Through All the Changing Scenes of Life." In *Trinity Hymnal, Rev. Ed,* (Atlanta-Philadelphia: Great Commission Publications).

Augustus M. Toplady, "Rock of Ages, Cleft for Me," In *Trinity Hymnal, Rev. Ed.,* (Atlanta-Philadelphia: Great Commission Publications, 2019).

Kevin J. Vanhoozer, *Hearers & Doers,* (Bellingham: Lexham Press, 2019).

Venantius H.C. Fortunatus, "Praise the Savior Now and Ever." In *Trinity Hymnal, Rev. Ed,* (Atlanta-Philadelphia: Great Commission Publications).

Westminster Shorter Catechism. Public Domain.

Max Zerwick, S.J. and Mary Grosvenor, *A Grammatical Analysis of the Greek New Testament*, (Roma: Editrice Pontifico Instituto Biblico, 1996 (1974)).

ABOUT WHITE BLACKBIRD BOOKS

White blackbirds are extremely rare, but they are real. They are blackbirds that have turned white over the years as their feathers have come in and out over and over again. They are a redemptive picture of something you would never expect to see but that has slowly come into existence over time.

There is plenty of hurt and brokenness in the world. There is the hopelessness that comes in the midst of lost jobs, lost health, lost homes, lost marriages, lost children, lost parents, lost dreams, loss.

But there also are many white blackbirds. There are healed marriages, children who come home, friends who are reconciled. There are hurts healed, children fostered and adopted, communities restored. Some would call these events entirely natural, but really they are unexpected miracles.

The books in this series are not commentaries, nor are they meant to be the final word. Rather, they are a collage of biblical truth applied to current times and places. The authors share their poverty and trust the Lord to use their words to strengthen and encourage his people. Consider these books as entries into the discussion.

May this series help you in your quest to know Christ as he is found in the Gospel through the Scriptures. May you look for and even expect the rare white blackbirds of God's redemption through Christ in your midst. May you be thankful when you look down and see your feathers have turned. May you also rejoice when you see that others have been unexpectedly transformed by Jesus.

ALSO BY WHITE BLACKBIRD BOOKS

A Year in the New Testament: Volumes 1 & 2

All Are Welcome: Toward a Multi-Everything Church

The Almost Dancer

Birth of Joy: Philippians

Choosing a Church: A Biblical and Practical Guide

Christ in the Time of Corona: Stories of Faith, Hope, and Love

Co-Laborers, Co-Heirs: A Family Conversation

The Crossroads of Adultery

Doing God's Work

Driven by Desire

EmbRACE: A Biblical Study on Justice and Race

Ever Light and Dark: Telling Secrets, Telling the Truth

Everything Is Meaningless? Ecclesiastes

Faithful Doubt: Habakkuk

Firstfruits of a New Creation

Heal Us Emmanuel: A Call for Racial Reconciliation, Representation, and

Follow whiteblackbirdbooks.pub for titles and releases.

Made in the USA
Monee, IL
17 September 2021